LITSTART

Literacy Strategies for Adult Reading Tutors

Second Edition, Revised

Ed Robson
Marsha DeVergilio
Donna DeButts

A Publication of Michigan Literacy, Inc.
Lansing, Michigan

— 1990 —

Library of Congress Catalog Card Number: 89-64316

Michigan Literacy, Inc.
c/o Library of Michigan
717 W. Allegan
P.O. Box 30007
Lansing, MI 48909
(517) 373-4451

The changing ideas about reading (including a new definition) have led to a need for a more comprehensive book for tutors and others interested in helping adults acquire basic reading skills.

The first edition, written by Pat Frey and the Michigan Method Training Committee (Linda Bejma, Candyce Williams, Donna DeButts, and Cathyrn Weiss), has aided thousands of tutors in assisting non-readers in developing literacy skills.

This revised edition reflects the continually changing trends in reading and literacy. Input came from tutors, students, tutor trainers, adult education teachers, reading specialists, and reading researchers. New concepts in this edition were field tested by literacy tutor trainers in Michigan.

With this edition, the goal of the authors was to produce a book that could be used to train volunteer tutors, as well as be a book that tutors and students could use together in their weekly sessions.

An index has been included in this revised edition to help tutors, trainers, and teaches located information more easily.

Robert D'Amico of RDA Creative Art Services, Inc. designed the page format of the book utilizing blocks of white space, larger type sizes, and exciting graphics to hold the reader's attention. Emphasis has been placed on readability. Strategies for reading, writing, and spelling have been arranged in an easy-to-use format.

The underlying principle of the entire book is: *Focus on the Reader as an Individual.* Each new reader offers a unique challenge to the tutor. Individualizing instruction is emphasized in each section.

The key to teaching someone to read is not so much in the techniques or the materials, but in an attitude of mutual cooperation and support between the tutor and the new reader.

E.R., M.D., D.D.
January, 1990

Michigan Department of Education
and Michigan Reading Association
for the New Definition of Reading.

Library of Michigan
for its support of the
literacy network in Michigan.

Michigan Department of Education,
Adult Extended Learning Services,
for providing support to volunteer
literacy programs in Michigan.

Literacy Volunteers of America (LVA)
and Laubach Literacy Action (LLA)
for their contribution to
tutor training methodology.

Macomb County Library
and the Library Cooperative of Macomb
for providing the resources to facilitate
the production of **LITSTART**.

Robert D'Amico
of RDA Creative Art Services, Inc.
for the art direction, design,
and production of **LITSTART**.

Pat Frey for her contributions
to the revised **LITSTART**.

Malloy Lithography, Inc.
for providing the resources to facilitate
the publication and distribution of **LITSTART**.

Literacy & Reading

Reading is the first step in breaking
out of the Maze of Illiteracy.

Section 1

LITERACY & READING

Reader + **Text** + **Context** = Reading

Reading is the first step in becoming functionally literate.

LITERACY & READING
An Overview

Defining Literacy

Historical
Being able to sign one's name

UNESCO, 1951
A person is literate who can, with understanding, both read and write a short, simple statement on his/her everyday life.

Military, since World War I
Completion of the 8th grade

Census Bureau, 1979
A person who has completed six or more years of schooling.

National Assessment of Education Progress (NAEP), 1986
Using printed and written information to function in society to achieve one's goals and to develop one's knowledge and potential.

World Congress, 2015

?

Literacy in America

America does well helping those at the bottom of the literacy scale; but has serious problems helping at the upper levels of literacy as job requirements and changes become increasingly more demanding.
It's like catching a moving train.

- Ninety percent of jobs require reading and writing for an average of two to three hours per day. High school seniors only read and write an average of of one to two hours per day.

- Four of five young adults (ages 21-25) cannot read a bus schedule.

Illiteracy Affects Our Future

Beyond the personal plight of each functionally illiterate adult, the problems of illiteracy have a direct bearing on us ALL. Illiteracy is changing society as we know it.

A Lifetime of Poverty

- Over $240 billion in lifetime earnings are forfeited by men, aged 25-40, who have less than high school level skills.

- It is estimated that the cost of illiteracy to business and the taxpayer is $20 billion per year. Five billion dollars in taxes go to support people receiving public assistance who are unemployable due to illiteracy.

Workers Needed!

- While unemployment rates fall, American industry still can't find enough employees with basic literacy skills to fill empty positions.

- Three-fourths of the unemployed do not have the basic reading skills to be trained for high-tech jobs. The availability of high-tech jobs will not solve unemployment problems.

- $225 billion is the estimated cost of nonproductivity, including losses attributable to crime.

A Remedial Society

- One-fourth of all army recruits are put into remedial classes so that they can understand training manuals written at a seventh-grade level.

- Many army instruction booklets for the use of weapons and equipment are printed in comic book form.

- One of every ten drivers on the highway cannot read road signs. (Their driving tests were read to them.)

- $6.6 billion are spent each year for prison maintenance for an estimated 260,000 inmates whose incarcerations are related to illiteracy.

A Voiceless & Faceless Nation

- One-third of the nation cannot vote.

- They cannot write a letter to their Senators, to their Representatives, or to the President.

- In an age of computers and robotics, illiteracy may mean the loss of the ability to work!

Illiteracy among Blacks and Hispanics is two to three times greater than the national average, producing even greater inequities in employment and income.

CAUTION
DANGER AHEAD!

The U.S. News forecasts that the decline
in reading skills will lead in two
decades to an elite, literate class of no
more than 30% of the population.

Unless We Reverse the Trend...

by the year 2000,
2 out of 3 American adults
will be functionally illiterate.

National, state, and local literacy
organizations are waging an all- out battle
on illiteracy. Their goal is help people
to gain the first step in becoming
functionally literate...
learning to read.

A New Definition of Reading

Reading is	
the process of constructing meaning	(Reading)
through the dynamic interaction	
among the reader's existing knowledge,	(Reader)
the information suggested by the written language,	(Text)
and the context of the reading situation.	(Context)

In other words:

$$\text{Reader} + \text{Text} + \text{Context} = \text{Reading}$$

The ultimate goal of reading instruction is the development of a reader who can flexibly and independently process written language for meaning.

Meaning that is constructed by a reader is dependent to a large extent on the relationship between the author's purpose for writing the text and the reader's purpose for reading. A reader will construct different meaning about nature from a poem, a textbook, or a novel.

The reader's ability to construct meaning about a particular topic is dependent upon the reader's background knowledge of that topic. A good reader activates background knowledge of a topic.

Background knowledge helps the reader to understand the passage. *What do I know?* It also sets purpose for reading. *What do I want to know?* Activating the reader's thinking helps the reader connect new information to information already possessed.

The psychological, physical, social, cultural, and linguistic characteristics of the reader interact with the reading task to influence the process. Understanding how adults learn is important in helping them learn how to read. **Adults bring a lifetime of experience to the learning situation.**

Developing Reading Skills

- A skilled reader learns to reason about written material using knowledge from everyday life.

- A skilled reader has developed the basic process in reading to the point where reading focuses on meaning, not on mechanics.

- A skilled reader is able to select and change reading strategies depending upon the purpose for reading, the nature of material, and level of understanding.

- The skilled reader is motivated to making reading a lifelong pursuit.

- A skilled reader has a self-concept of being a good reader.

To help someone become a skilled reader, instruction must provide a student with knowledge about different situations and the ability to apply this knowledge in a flexible manner. As reading ability increases, the reader is constantly refining the way text is approached. The reader becomes more knowledgeable in selecting strategies for achieving reading goals.

To help adults become skilled readers, a multisensory method is usually best. The instruction is presented in several modalities. Frequently, kinesthetic (movement) and tactile (touch) stimulations are used along with visual and auditory modalities.

Section 2 will discuss the needs of the adult reader in detail.

The Reader

The Key to a
Brighter Future

Section 2
THE READER

Reader + Text + Context = Reading

*The **reader** is the key ingredient in
the reading process.*

THE READER

The reader is the most important factor in the reading process. Your understanding of the adult new reader will increase your effectiveness in the reading partnership.

Adults come to reading with diverse backgrounds:

- a bricklayer from an urban area
- a retired miner from a rural area
- a laid-off auto plant worker
- a foreign-born seamstress
- a single mother looking for a job to get off ADC

Adults come to reading with diverse abilities:

- can only sign his name
- can read headlines in the newspaper
- can recognize several letters of the alphabet
- can read simple everyday materials
- can read well in her native language but not English

Adults come to reading with diverse goals:

- a parent wants to read to a child
- a man wants to become a church deacon
- a widow wants to be able to write checks
- a dropout wants to return to school
- a welder wants to read blueprints
- an auto worker wants to read his union's contract
- an inmate wants to read the Bible

MEET DON, EDDIE, AND MARIA

Don, Eddie, and Maria are just three of thousands of students working with tutors across the United States. They and their tutors have decided to share their experiences with you, so that you can understand, first hand, what learning to read, as an adult, is all about.

Getting to know them will help you put the new things you are learning about reading, into practice. Don, Eddie, and Maria appear throughout LITSTART.

DON: A Beginning Reader

**"I'm tired of bluffing it!
I'm frustrated.....I'm ready to learn.
Through adult education, I found
I'm not too old to learn."**

Don is 41 and twice divorced. He has two sons, not living with him. He is reading at a beginning level and his goal is to be able to read labels, books, and mail for his job. He works in a pet store and breeds dogs. He is anxious to make fast progress. Don graduated from a special education program. His immediate need is to be able to write his address from memory. Don is presently enrolled in an adult basic education classroom. His teacher has suggested he get a tutor from the Literacy Project.

EDDIE: An Intermediate Reader

" I know if I could just read better, I could do anything I want. Just like the person in the television ad, I want to be successful. With my tutor's help, I know I will succeed."

Eddie is 31 and single. He is reading at an intermediate level. His goal is to get a better job, perhaps in skilled trade. Eddie works long hours as a dishwasher. As a youngster, he was kept out of school to work on the farm. He is articulate. He enjoys meeting people. He has a good sense of humor and likes rock music, parties, and girls. Eddie lives alone, and he would like his own saving and checking accounts. He has a driver's license, but has never been able to take the written test. Eddie is able to make simple repairs on his car but has difficulty reading the owner's manual. Eddie heard about the program on TV from Project Literacy United States (PLUS)

MARIA: An Advanced Reader

"I'm so excited that I will be able to read to my grandchildren. I remember how I enjoyed having my grandmother read to me."

Maria is 54 years old. She is divorced, has one son and three grandchildren, and is reading at the advanced level. Her goal is to obtain her driver's license. Maria is an energetic, independent, cheerful woman. She works in a factory and plans to retire early and travel. She enjoys gardening and cooking. She heard about the Literacy Project from her sister who drove her to the library for her first tutoring session. She would love to be able to read to her grandchildren. Maria has a slight hearing loss.

Teaching adults to read is **different** from teaching children. Adult students know a lot about the world. This knowledge affects all aspects of the reading process.

**BACKGROUND
KNOWLEDGE**

- Most adults have a sense of language. They know the pattern of language and how it should sound. Some may be familiar with language and reading to the point that they know print is "talk, written down."

- Adults have a wide range of knowledge through a variety of experiences. They know about their jobs, their families, music, sports, politics, and "101 other things." This wealth of knowledge should be utilized in the reading process.

PRIORITIES

Adult students may have urgent survival needs or other important goals. Personal goals should have top priority.

CONTROL

Adults are used to making decisions. Respect students' opinions, preferences, and priorities. Encourage students to be involved in the selection of books and activities.

MOTIVATION

Adult students have an interest and desire to learn to read. Success helps maintain motivation. Showing students what has been accomplished toward reading goals will keep them going.

TIME

Students, like you, have responsibilities that restrict time. This means priorities must be chosen carefully. Use your weekly time together wisely.

COMMUNICATION

Clear communication is essential. Always check with students to be sure that you are being understood.

> *Any of the factors below can influence the adult reader's ability to learn.*

Environmental Factors

Readers who squint or tip back their chairs may be bothered by glare. Some people have trouble reading in fluorescent light. Try natural or incandescent light if possible. Sunglasses or a visor may help.

LIGHT

If your student is used to background noise (radio or TV) at home, a radio turned on low may help concentration. If your student needs quiet, close the door.

SOUND

If possible, adjust the temperature to suit your student.

TEMPERATURE

Physical Factors

While some people like to sit at a desk when they read, others like to lean back and put their feet up. Ask how your student likes to read at home and try to accommodate that style.

POSITION

Students whose eyes or hands tire quickly after reading or writing build up muscle strength gradually. Start with only a few minutes and build from there. Also, a student with eyestrain may need a vision checkup.

MUSCLE STRENGTH

Arrange for breaks to meet your student's needs.

INTAKE

If possible, arrange your sessions in the morning for a "morning person" and in the evening for a "night person."

TIME OF DAY

Your student's limit for sitting may be shorter than yours. Check regularly to see if your student needs to stretch.

MOBILITY

VISUAL Learners:

- Recall words after seeing them a few times.
- Prefer directions that are written.
- Can concentrate on visual tasks despite visual distractions.
- Remember and understand words accompanied by pictures and graphs.
- Discriminate between letters that look alike (m/n) and words that look alike (full/fill).
- Do not confuse the order of letters (stop/spot).

Implications for tutoring:

For a visual student, use written instructions, not just oral ones. A Language Experience Story may work better than phonics. Use pictures and charts if possible and make pictures out of words or letters.

AUDITORY Learners:

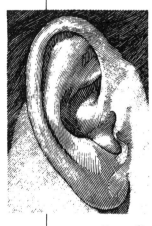

- Recall words after hearing them a few times.
- Prefer oral instructions.
- Can concentrate on listening despite auditory distractions.
- Use appropriate vocabulary and sentence structure.
- Discriminate between words that sound alike (cat/cot) and letters that sound alike (t/d).
- Blend sounds quickly to form words.
- Can retain the story line while sounding out words.

Implications for tutoring:

Use tapes, radio, discussions, and verbal explanations with an auditory student. Read aloud to student. Tapes of words may be better than flash cards. Echo reading may help. Have student listen to a tape of a book while reading it. Give oral instructions, not just written ones.

KINESTHETIC Learners:

- Recall words after writing them a few times.
- Move smoothly, rhythmically, and freely.
- Recall words from signs seen on a trip.
- Recall words more easily when walking or pacing.
- Remember the feelings of a story better than the details.

TACTILE Learners:

- Recall words after typing them a few times.
- Excel at crafts such as sewing or making models.
- Hold a pen or pencil correctly.
- Write legibly and proportionately.
- Recall words after touching the object they represent or using them in a game.

Implications for tutoring:

Students with strong tactile and kinesthetic skills may benefit by using Scrabble tiles, alphabet cut-outs (made of wood, sandpaper, or textured material), or lettered dice to make words. Games that let the student identify the answer by manipulating, rather than saying it, may help. Computers and the Experience Story are excellent tools.

28

Some students have special needs when learning to read. They may have hearing, vision, or learning problems, or they may be learning English as a second language. You can use the same techniques with special reading students that you use with other students.

STUDENTS WITH HEARING PROBLEMS

Symptoms:

- Talking loudly
- Asking you to repeat
- Frequently not "remembering" what you said
- Misunderstanding you
- Turning one ear toward you when you talk
- Not hearing you (when not looking directly at you)

If you suspect your student has a hearing problem:

- Encourage the student to have hearing checked
- Enunciate clearly
- Speak loudly, but don't yell
- Sit on the student's "good side"
- Make sure the student is aware when you start to speak
- Ask the student to repeat things back to you

" My tutor discovered that I had a hearing loss because I was not hearing the *endings* on words. Now I have a hearing aid and my spelling has really improved."

STUDENTS WITH VISION PROBLEMS

Symptoms:

- Squinting
- Holding the book too close
- Bending low over the table
- Holding the book far away
- Headache
- Eye fatigue
- Inability to read small print

If you think your student may have a vision problem:

- Encourage the student to have vision checked
- Ask the student to tell you when the print is too small to read
- Work in a well lit area
- Encourage the student to position the book where it can be seen best
- Check with the library for large-print books

" Because I had never really read before, I found that I was having trouble reading the small print. A pair of inexpensive reading glasses has really helped."

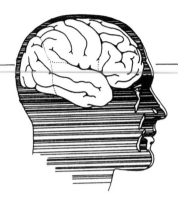

STUDENTS WITH LEARNING DISABILITIES

A learning disability is a learning problem associated with the way the brain processes information.

Students with learning disabilities may experience difficulty:

- Staying on task

- Keeping their place on the page

- Reversing letters or sequencing

- Understanding what is read

- Recalling what is read

- Learning and remembering sight words

- Time sequencing (in what order do things occur)

- Forming letters when writing

- Communicating in a written form

People with learning disabilities have trouble seeing letters correctly, hearing sounds correctly, or writing correctly even though their eyes, ears, and muscles work fine. **Students with learning disabilities just learn differently.**

People with learning disabilities usually display average or above average intelligence. They often have enviable talents in other areas.

DYSLEXIA

Dyslexia is a type of learning disability. True dyslexia is not curable, but it is manageable. A dyslexic person can learn to read in spite of seeing things scrambled.

Leonardo da Vinci

> A person with dyslexia may see:
>
> ## Saw the bog unber the huose?
>
> instead of:
>
> ## Was the dog under the house?

Some dyslexics have been very successful: Thomas Edison, Albert Einstein, General Patton, Rodin, Woodrow Wilson, Winston Churchill, Nelson Rockefeller, Hans Christian Anderson, and Leonardo da Vinci.

When working with dyslexic students, use all avenues of learning.

Albert Einstein

- Focus on the student's strengths to compensate for the weaknesses.

- Focus on comprehension. True dyslexics learn to cope by noticing when something doesn't make sense. Then they simply reread.

- Focus on a small section of text. It may be necessary to cover up all but the line or section you are working on to reduce visual distraction.

- Focus on meeting the student's needs. It may be necessary to rewrite the materials being used into a format better suited to the student.

Check with your literacy coordinator for other resources.

歡迎　Welkom
Velkommen　Benvenuto
Bienvenue　Bienvenido
Välkomna　Bem-vindo
ようこそ　Willkommen

STUDENTS LEARNING ENGLISH

Students who grew up speaking any language other than English are known as ESL (English as a Second Language) students. For them, English is a foreign language.

Teaching spoken English is beyond the scope of this book. Check with your literacy coordinator to find out if ESL classes or ESL tutoring workshops are available in your area.

If ESL classes do exist, encourage your student to attend. If the student can work with you and attend classes, progress will be much faster.

In working with an ESL student, be especially polite so as not to offend the student inadvertently. Touching, standing too close, wearing certain clothing, talking loudly, discussing politics, or using first names may be taboo in your student's culture.

You should not be offended if the student appears impolite to you. Perhaps avoiding eye contact is polite behavior in the student's culture. Keep your mind open.

Pre-Reading Checklist for ESL Tutors

	YES	NO
1. Does the student understand what is said?	❏	❏
2. Can the student follow directions given orally?	❏	❏
3. Does the student see likenesses and differences in letters, words, and word patterns?	❏	❏
4. Can the student hear the differences and similarities in initial consonant sounds?	❏	❏
5. Can the student recognize words which rhyme?	❏	❏
6. Is the student able to visually track from left to right?	❏	❏
7. Is the student able to recognize common word meanings in spoken context?	❏	❏
8. Does the student understand that print stands for or represents speech?	❏	❏

If you were able to check yes to most of the questions above, your ESL student is ready to begin learning to read.

The native speaker of English is expected to possess a minimum speaking vocabulary of 2,500 words to be successful in learning to read.

TIPS FOR WORKING WITH ESL STUDENTS

- You can use the same techniques as you would for any student.

- Learning English includes learning idioms and expressions. Treat them like new vocabulary. Limit your use of idioms if your student is struggling.

    > Everyday English is filled with thousands of phrases that are meaningless when each word is defined separately.

    > English contains many modern expressions and slang.

    > Examples include: call up, come over, up to you, call off, run into, ripped off, fool around, in hot water, kick the bucket.

- Check frequently for word meanings. ESL students sometimes say they understand just to be polite.

- Use Language Experience Stories. This will help you to understand the limits of the student's vocabulary.

- When working on word families, do not use nonsense words with the ESL student.

Reading for Meaning

Comprehension is the
Light at the End of the Tunnel

Section 3

READING
FOR MEANING

Reader + Text + Context = **Reading**

*The skilled reader brings many strategies
to the reading task to help construct meaning.*

READING FOR MEANING

Text comes in different forms requiring diverse comprehension skills

Learning to read is more than just saying the words written on the page. Without meaning (comprehension), the words are just marks on the page. The skilled reader has learned to approach text with a variety of skills.

The skilled reader picks the strategy (or strategies) to use depending on:

- The reader's **reason for reading** the text.
- The reader's **prior knowledge** of the topic.
- The reader's **interest** in reading the text.
- The reader's understanding of the **vocabulary** in the text.

Reading is bringing meaning to and getting meaning from text.

Read Passage A and answer the question that follows.

Passage A

We may measure and coordinate omnirationally, energetically, arithmetically, vectorially, topologically, and energy-quantum-wise in terms of the tetrahedron.

How do you coordinate omnirationally?

_____

_____

	Yes	No
Did reading Passage A spark your interest?	❑	❑
Do you have prior knowledge about the topic?	❑	❑
Did you have a real purpose for reading Passage A?	❑	❑
Did you understand the vocabulary in Passage A?	❑	❑

What strategies did you use to help you read Passage A?

_____

_____

_____

Did reading occur?	❑	❑

Now read Passage B and answer the question that follows.

Passage B

Almxxx evxxx yxxr, Mrs. Crooks climbs up a mxxxxxxn whxch is ovxx fourtxxx thxxxxxx fxxt hixx. Mrs. Crooks xx ninexx-one yxxxx old.

What does Mrs. Crooks do?

_____

_____

	Yes	No
Did reading Passage B spark your interest?	❑	❑
Do you have prior knowledge about the topic?	❑	❑
Did you have a real purpose for reading Passage B?	❑	❑
Did you understand the vocabulary in Passage B?	❑	❑

What strategies did you use to help you read Passage B?

_____

_____

_____

Did reading occur?	❑	❑

With Passage A, skilled readers can use their decoding skills to sound out the words. Background knowledge about the topic is missing or weak. Some of the words make sense, but perhaps not in the context that they are used in the passage. **For most people, reading does not occur.**

With Passage B, skilled readers can use their knowledge of reading, their decoding skills, their sense of "wordness" in English, and their prior knowledge of the topic to figure out what the passage says. **For almost all readers, reading occurs.**

Skilled readers have strategies that new readers must learn in order to be successful in dealing with the variety of texts and reading tasks that occur during a lifetime.

This section of **LITSTART** will provide you with strategies to help bring *meaning to reading* for your student.

The essence of tutoring is sharing what you know about reading with a student.

Remember

Comprehension increases when you:

Choose something to read that sparks your student's interest.

Talk about the passage to be read to find out what your student already knows about the topic.

Ask questions to set a purpose for reading the passage.

Talk about the new vocabulary, before and after reading.

Reading Strategies

For each Reading Strategy, you will find:

- **Strategy Name**
  A handle to help you and your student remember the strategy

- **Rationale**
  The reason for using the strategy

- **Materials**
  Supplies and texts needed for the strategy

- **Procedure**
  The step-by-step method

Most of the strategies will be appropriate for all students. We have tried to identify which strategies would be appropriate for beginning, intermediate, advanced, or English as a Second Language students.

Some strategies are best used with materials that the student can use independently, but most are designed to be used with material at the student's instructional level. The student's instructional level is where the student must have assistance, but can work with you without becoming frustrated or discouraged.

If you find that a strategy does not work for you or your student, don't use it. You may discover ways to modify the strategies.

Every student is different. The key to being a successful tutor is being flexible.

Strategy 1

Skip, Guess, Sound, Ask...

Rationale: Provides student with a method of using context clues to decode unknown words.

Materials: Reading passage at student's instructional level.

Note: Some of the passage may be difficult.

Procedure: The tutor shares with the student the following strategy that good readers use.

SKIP "When I come to a word I don't know, I skip it and read to the end of the sentence."

GUESS "Sometimes when I get to the end of the sentence, I can guess the word from the rest of the sentence."

SOUND "Sometimes I use phonics to sound out the word."

ASK "Some words don't follow any of the rules, then I ask someone." Advanced readers may look the word up in the dictionary.

Oral Model

Strategy 2

Rationale:
1. Aids in developing sight word recognition.

2. Provides students the opportunity to hear standard English aloud.

3. Helps student to develop the feel of phrasing in English (an excellent strategy for ESL students)

4. Introduces students to new vocabulary in context.

5. Provides motivation for independent student reading.

6. Uses repetition to increase fluency.

Materials: Reading passage at independent/instructional level. Pick a topic of interest to the student.

Procedure:
1. Tutor reads aloud and student follows silently.

2. Discuss the passage.

3. Tutor encourages the student to read the passage. It may be necessary for the student to reread the passage several times for fluency and comprehension to occur.

Strategy 3 — Reading Together

Rationale:
1. Increases student's confidence when reading aloud.
2. Helps to impress the words into the student's memory.

Materials:
Text that is of interest to student and is near the instructional level.

Procedure:
1. Tutor sits to the **right** of the student.
2. Tutor and student read together.

   The tutor should read one or two syllables ahead of the student.

Echo Reading

Strategy 4

Rationale:
1. Increases sight word recognition.
2. Increases confidence reading aloud.
3. Models phrasing and pronunciation.

   (This strategy is good for ESL students and beginning students.)

Materials: Reading passage at student's instructional level

Procedure:
1. Tutor reads a sentence from the passage.

2. Student reads the same sentence imitating the tutor's stress and intonation.

48

Strategy 5   **Taped Readings**

Rationale:
1. Allows the student to work independently between sessions.
2. Increases sight word mastery.

Materials:
tape recorder

blank tape

reading passage that is of interest to student

Procedure:
1. Tutor makes a tape of reading passage.
2. Student listens to the tape while following the reading passage.
3. Student reads aloud slightly faster than tape. The tape becomes an echo.
4. The student reads the passage without the tape.
5. Student can repeat steps 2 through 4 as needed.

" I Think That..."

Strategy 6

Rationale: Student learns how a successful reader interacts with text.

Materials: Passage at student's instructional level.

Note: Some of the passage may be difficult.

Procedure:
1. The tutor reads part of the selected passage aloud.

2. Tutor then processes the passage aloud for the student by:

- Making predictions: "I think that _____will probably happen..."

- Describing mental images: "When I read this, it makes me think of..."

- Showing when to reread or ask questions: "...This just doesn't make sense."

Strategy 7 "Just Hummin' Along"

Rationale:

1. Provides reading practice by presenting words in a meaningful context. Student is able to form a bridge between the music and the text.

2. Allows student to hear colloquial language. (Excellent strategy for use with ESL students.)

Materials:

cassette tapes or records
player for tapes or records
sheet music or song book of lyrics

Procedure:

1. Have student listen to the tape or record.

2. Student follows along with a written copy of the song.

   This can be repeated as often as necessary until student can read sheet music without tape or record.

> Memories, like the corners of my mind
> Misty watercolor memories
> Of the way we were
> Scattered pictures
> Of the smiles we left behind
> Smiles we gave to one another
> For the way we were

From the Columbia Picture, Rastar Production,
"The Way We Were" © 1973

"Tell Me What You've Read"

Strategy 8

Rationale:
1. Develops student's ability to read silently for meaning.
2. Increases motivation to read independently.

Materials: Two passages at the student's independent level.

Procedure:
1. Tutor and student independently read a selected passage.
2. Tutor and student share the contents of passages read.
3. Tutor and student trade passages to read.
4. Tutor and student share ideas on the second reading.

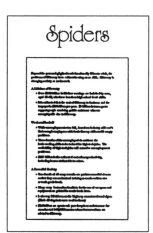

52

Strategy 9   Let's Find Out

Rationale:
1. Activates the student's prior knowledge of the topic selected.
2. Sets purpose for reading.
3. A strategy for non-fiction reading.

Materials:
Non-fiction passage from a textbook at the student's instructional level.

Procedure:
1. Brainstorm: What do we already know ?

   _____

   _____

   _____

2. Brainstorm: What do we want to find out?

   _____

   _____

   _____

3. Brainstorm (after reading): What did we find out about the topic from the reading? What do we still need to find out?

   _____

   _____

   _____

Road Map for Reading Enjoyment — Strategy 10

Rationale:

1. Gives the student a direction or purpose for reading.

2. Provides the student an opportunity to practice critical thinking skills.

Materials:

Short fictional passage appropriate for the student's interests and ability levels.

Procedure:

1. Before reading the passage, both tutor and student discuss the reading and make predictions using their own background knowledge.

2. Tutor and student read passage silently.

3. The tutor and student generate new questions and predictions based on the passage read.

4. Tutor and student discuss the passage, and either accept or reject predictions based upon what they already know and what's in the text.

Sample questions for post reading activity:

- Is this a good title?

- What do you think should have been included?

- What was the author trying to tell us?

- How do you feel after reading this?

- How do you think the author felt when writing this story?

Strategy 11

Word Web

Rationale: Helps the student prepare to read new material by activating prior knowledge.

Materials: paper

pencil

text to be read that is at student's interest and instructional level.

Procedure: 1. Tutor prepares a list of words from the reading passage.

biscuit	Minnesota
banks	Mississippi River
Russia	dairy
four	three

2. Student predicts how the words are related.

Predictions:

1. Biscuits are made in Minnesota and Russia.
2. Water from the Mississippi River is used to make the biscuits.
3. Three biscuits in Russia cost four dollars.
4. Dairy cows love biscuits.
5. People save their biscuits in banks.

Prediction Web

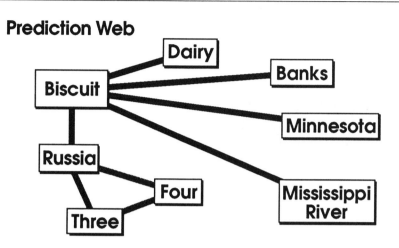

3. Student reads passage.

Reading:

The Ready-Made Biscuit Company is located in Minnesota on the banks of the Mississippi River. The company makes the biggest biscuits in the world. Each one is four inches wide and three inches high. Ready-Made biscuits are sold all over the world, even in Russia. You can buy these world-famous biscuits in your local dairy case.

4. Student compares predictions with actual reading.

5. Student revises predictions.

Revised Predictions:
1. Biscuits are made in Minnesota.
2. Biscuits are sold in Russia.
3. The biscuits are three by four inches.
4. The company is located on the banks of the Mississippi River.
5. The biscuits can be found in the dairy case.

Strategy 12 — *Summary Reading*

Rationale: Summarizing is a key strategy and a necessary study skill for good readers.

Materials: Text appropriate for student's instructional/ independent level and interest.

Procedure:
1. Tutor and student both read short passage silently.
2. Tutor summarizes or explains the text by saying:

"To me the passage seems to be saying..."

"What do you think?"

"I would like to rename the passage... "

"What would you call it?"

Questioning Partners

Strategy 13

Rationale:

1. Models reading for a purpose using prediction.

2. Allows student to self-assess comprehension.

Materials:

Text that is of interest to the student and at the student's instructional level

Procedure:

1. Tutor and student each silently read the same passage.

2. Tutor asks student a question about the passage.

3. Student then asks tutor a question.

4. Tutor models questioning strategies such as prediction or inference.

> Joe and Harry like to play baseball. They play every day after school in the empty lot next to their apartment building. Joe plays shortstop. Harry is the catcher. The other players on the team live in the same apartment building.

Student: Where do they play baseball? **(Fact)**

Tutor: How old do you think Joe and Harry are? **(Inference)**

Strategy 14

S Q 4 R
*(Survey, Question,
Read, Recite, Review, Write)*

Rationale: Study plan to help the student become a more effective reader. Requires the student to:

- Ask questions.
- Make predictions.
- Set purpose.
- Check comprehension.

Materials: Textbook written at instructional level

Procedure:

1. **Survey :**
   a. Look over the title and definitions.
   b. What do I already know or want to know?
   c. Look at pictures or graphs.
   d. Read summary or introduction.

2. **Question:**
   a. Formulate questions during survey.
   b. Write down words that are new and guess at meaning from text.

3. **Read Actively:** Read to find answers.

4. **Recite:**
   a. Put passage in your own words.
   b. Answer questions.

5. **Review:** Reread to find unanswered questions.

6. **Write:** Write summary or outline, etc.

Story Map

Rationale: Informs student how fiction stories are constructed.

Materials: Short story appropriate for student's interest and ability

Procedure: Have student read story silently and then with tutor's help fill in the blanks on the map.

Mary lives in a small town in Lakeville, Michigan. Mary is just sixteen years old and is learning to drive. She is a very nervous driver. On the way to school, Mary had an accident. She did not see the stop sign at the corner of Oak and Maple. She hit Mr. O'Reilly, the mayor of Lakeville. Mary had good insurance. All of the mayor's hospital bills were covered. Mary is glad that the mayor will be OK.

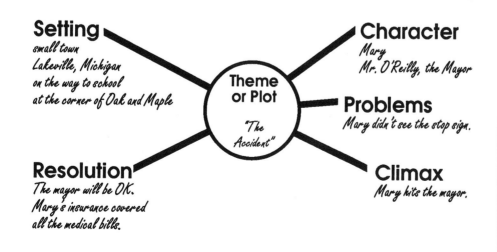

Setting
small town
Lakeville, Michigan
on the way to school
at the corner of Oak and Maple

Character
Mary
Mr. O'Reilly, the Mayor

Theme or Plot
"The Accident"

Problems
Mary didn't see the stop sign.

Resolution
The mayor will be OK.
Mary's insurance covered all the medical bills.

Climax
Mary hits the mayor.

Strategy 16   *Don't Get Lost*

Rationale: Helps students with vision problems keep their place on the page.

Materials: Black construction paper lines.

Procedure: Have student place lines under text as he/she reads.

It was a dark and stormy night.

the sky. It was followed by the crashing sound of thunder.

It was a dark and stormy night. Suddenly, a bolt of lightning lit up

crashing sound of thunder.

Fill in the Blanks

Strategy 17

Rationale: Helps student develop predicting skills by reading in context.

Materials: Short sentences with some words missing.

Procedure:

1. Copy sentences onto lined paper leaving a blank for the word to be supplied by the student.

2. Have the student read each sentence and predict the missing word.

3. With very beginning students, it may be necessary to supply alternate choices and have the student select the correct word.

(This exercise can be made for the beginning, intermediate, or advanced level student.)

Examples:

Beginning: The boy _____ home.
              (ran, rap)

The boy r_n home.
(a, i)

Intermediate: This _____ a good book.

The _____ is black and barks at the door.

Advanced: Mary _____ to the store to _____ milk, eggs, and butter.

Strategy 18

Language Experience

Rationale: Tutor and student can generate a reading text using the student's prior knowledge, vocabulary, and language patterns.

Materials:
paper

pencil

word cards

carbon paper

Procedure:

1. Talk:
Student and tutor converse on a topic of interest to the student.

2. Write:
Tutor writes down some of the student's comments.

3. Read:
Tutor and student practice reading the passage. At first, the tutor reads passage to clarify information. Then tutor and student read passage together.

Options:
- Have student read passage independently.
- Make a carbon copy of the stories for student and tutor files.
- Make word cards to practice new words.
- Create a *"Fill in the Blanks"* exercise (see Strategy 17).

My sister and I are very close. I talk

| sister |

to her on the telephone every weekend.

She lives in Florida. When we were

young, she would always take me to the

movies on Saturday. I wish she lived

closer to me.

| telephone | | talk |

| young | | take | | closer |

A
Language
Experience
Story

by Eddie

Strategy 19

Mapping (Pre-Reading)

Rationale:
1. Activates the student's prior knowledge of the topic.
2. Provides a system of organization for information.
3. Helps set purpose for reading.

Materials:
passage to be read
paper
pencil

Procedure:
1. Student and tutor discuss topic.
2. Tutor writes the key idea in the center of the paper.
3. The student and tutor brainstorm information about the key idea.
4. After reading the passage, the student and tutor revise the map.

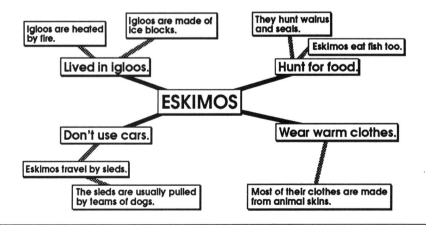

Mapping (Post-Reading)

Strategy 20

Rationale: Provides the student with a way to organize and retain information for later use.

Materials: passage to be read

paper

pencil

Procedure:
1. Student and tutor read the passage.

2. Tutor writes the key idea in the center of the paper.

3. The student supplies information remembered from the story.

4. The tutor writes this information on the map.

5. The tutor supplies information from the story and adds to the map.

6. Repeat steps 3 through 5, as needed.

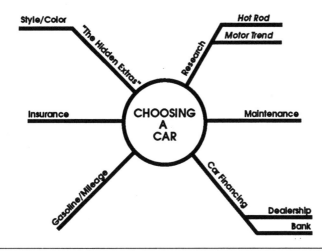

66

Readers Use A Variety of Keys to Unlock Text

Phonics • Word Families • Sight Words

Section 4

THE KEYS TO UNLOCKING TEXT

Reader + Text + Context = Reading

*Sight words, phonics, and word families are three keys that successful readers use to unlock **text**.*

THE KEYS TO UNLOCKING TEXT

Reading, for the skilled reader, is an almost automatic process. Emphasis is placed on meaning, not the mechanics of reading. The skilled reader uses various KEYS to unlock text. These keys have been used by the reader so often that the reader is unaware of using them.

For the new reader, words and letters are just marks on the page. The new reader must acquire the KEYS FOR UNLOCKING TEXT:

Sight Words—learning words as a single unit.

Phonics—learning words by combining sounds.

Word Families—learning words by recognizing common patterns.

There are many different ways to teach letter/word identification to adult beginning readers. Some tutors use Language Experience Activities; some use a published adult reading series. Adults should be encouraged to attempt to identify unknown words in the context of a reading passage and to use meaning as a check for correct word identification.

The following outline is only a suggestion for a possible sequence for word identification skills, and the tutor is encouraged to adapt instruction to the specific needs of the student.

Beginning Word Identification Skills:

- Beginning Sight Words (page 227)
- Initial consonant sounds (page 184)
- Beginning Word Families (page 192)
- Use of context with the above skills to decode unknown words

Intermediate Word Identification Skills:

- Intermediate Sight Words (page 227)
- 100 Most Frequent Words (page 229)
- Known words with endings -s, -ed, -ing
- Blends and digraphs (page 187 and page 191)
- Intermediate Word Families with long and short vowel combinations (page 198)
- Use of context and the above skills to decode unknown words

Advanced Word Identification Skills:

- Advanced Sight Words (page 228)
- Advanced Word Families with more complex vowel combinations (page 215)
- Compound words and contractions (page 219 and page 230)
- Syllabication rules (page 92)
- Use of context and the above skills to decode unknown words

The reading vocabulary consists of words recognized in print instantly. Tutors will want to help new readers develop an increasing independent reading vocabulary. Any of the keys (phonics, sight words, word families) can help build that vocabulary.

Sight words allow the new reader to look at a word as a single unit. The reader is able to analyze its shape and special features. Using the word in context will help move that word into the reading vocabulary. Words that are phonetically inconsistent are better learned using the sight method. Any word that creates problems for the student should be learned by sight.

Procedure for increasing sight vocabulary

1. Put the word to be learned on a flashcard.

2. Use the word in a sentence.
   Write the sentence on the back of the card.

3. Have the student practice saying, spelling, and writing the word.

4. Review the word regularly.

| friends | Tom and Mark are my **friends**. |

Tips

- Select words to study from the student's reading.
- Practice selected words in context to reinforce meaning.
- Have student match sight word cards to words in a story.
- Have student look through a newspaper or magazine article for a given sight word and circle it when found.
- Attach a picture to the word card to ease comprehension especially for foreign students.
- Mark the card each time the student recognizes the word instantly; retire it after 3 to 5 correct responses.

Readers have four vocabularies: listening, speaking, writing, and reading.

There are several options for introducing consonant sounds:

- Select a published adult beginner book that teaches consonant sounds. Supplement the activities in the book as needed with extra words

- Develop a file or list of words to help the student practice and remember the consonant sounds:

1. *Generate a list of words that begin with a selected letter.* You can do this yourself before the lesson or together with your student during your lesson. Any reading selection can be used as a source of words to start the list. Also, consider words of personal significance to the student such as names of family members, local streets, city, state, and employer.

2. *Help the student read the list and isolate the sound at the beginning of the words.*

3. *Have the student choose a favorite KEY WORD as a memory aid.*

4. *Write the student's selected key word at the top of the list.* If possible, include a sketch or picture of the object or action represented by the key word.

b

bike
ball
baby
book
bird
boy
bottle
bat

B

Bob
Bonnie
Baker St.

Practicing Sounds

After introducing a sound, provide practice for your student either by following an instructional series or by developing your own exercises.

Here are some examples:

I will say a word. If you hear the /b/ sound (for example) on the beginning of the word, say "yes." If you do not hear the /b/ sound, say "no."

I will say a sound. You say the letter that makes that sound.

I will say a word. You say the letter you hear at the beginning of the word.

I will say a word. The word will begin with one of these two (or more) letters. You say the letter.

I will show you some letters (make flash cards). You say the sound (or the key word and the sound). Sort cards into two piles as the student gets right or wrong answers. Review the ones missed.

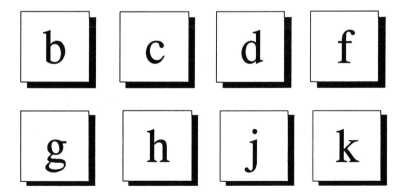

Suggestions

- Have the student write the letter, rather than say it.

- Have the student identify the ending sound, rather than the beginning sound.

- Have the student identify both the beginning and ending sounds.

- For beginning students, try to avoid blends: use "fee" but not "free" and "sing" but not "sting."

- Give the student credit for identifying the correct SOUND even when the spelling does not match.

> City begins with an S sound.
> Phone begins with an F sound.
> Chef begins with an SH sound.
>
> Cars ends with a Z sound.
> Love ends with a V sound.
> Laugh ends with an F sound.

- Watch for patterns in your student's errors. If your student consistently confuses two sounds, develop a practice list for just those two sounds.

This information is a reference for you on consonant sounds.

B: It usually produces a consistent sound. The B can be silent (comb, subtle).

C: This letter has two sounds, /k/ and /s/. Since it does not sound like its name, it is difficult for beginners to learn.

> When C is followed by an E, I, or Y, that C will sound like an S, otherwise known as a soft C. This rule is over 99% true!

Examples:

CE: face, cent, receive, ceiling, chance, innocence
CI: city, circle, circumstance
CY: fancy, racy, bicycle, cyclone, cymbal, cyst, democracy

D: Produces a consistent sound. The D is silent in the word Wednesday.

F: It's a consistent sound that can be sustained.

G: It does not sound like its name, and it forms special combinations. It can be silent (ought, gnat, sign).

> When G is followed by an E, I, or Y, that G will sound like a J. Such a G is known as a soft G.

This rule is not as reliable as the soft C rule. Some notable exceptions are: get, give, and girl.

Note:
The letter U is often used to **protect** the G from the softening effects of a vowel (guess, fatigue, guide, guitar, guy).

When C is followed by an E, I, or Y, that C will sound like an S. This rule is over 99% true!

Examples:

GE: age, orange, refrigerate, germ, fudge, general, George
GI: giraffe, gin, giant, ginger, region, religious, magi
GY: cagy, gyrate, gym, gypsy, Egypt, biology, apology

H: It does not sound like its name. It is often silent (school, honest, John), and it often combines with other letters to make new sounds (ch, gh, ph, sh, th, wh).

J: It produces a consistent sound (same sound as the soft G).

K: Its sound is consistent (same sound as the hard C). It is almost always silent in the combination of KN (know, knot).

L: Like the letter R, it often blends with other consonants. It can be silent (salmon, half).

M: It is easy to make consistently, and it can be sustained.

N: Its consistent sound can be sustained. It can be silent (hymn, autumn).

P: It produces consistent sound. It can be silent (psalm, coup, receipt).

Q: It usually combines with a U to form the sound KWUH, but sometimes the U is silent and the Q sounds like a K (unique, liquor), and occasionally there is no U (Iraq, qiana).

R: When R follows a vowel, it changes the vowel sound. It often combines with other consonants to form blends. Some students, especially foreign-born, have trouble making the R sound.

S: It is a sound that can be sustained. It is the same sound as the soft C. The S often sounds like Z at the end of a word (rose, cars). The S can be silent (corps, debris, island).

T: T is a consistent sound. It can be silent (depot, often, castle).

V: It's a consistent sound that can be sustained.

W: Does not sound like its name. It often serves as a vowel. It can be silent (sword, answer, who), and it is almost always silent in the combination WR (write, wrap).

X: X makes the **/ks/** sound at the end of words such as box and six. It may sound like **/z/** at the beginning of words like xylophone or Xerox or may say its name as in x-ray.

Y: At the end of a one-syllable word, it makes the long i sound (my, cry). At the end of a two-syllable word, it makes the long e sound (baby, city).

Z: It's a consistent sound that can be sustained.

Consonant Word List

a		n	name
b	bird	o	
c	car	p	piano
d	door	q	quart
e		r	rose
f	fish	s	start
g	gas	t	toe
h	hello	u	
i		v	vase
j	jello	w	wagon
k	kite	x	tax
l	label	y	yarn
m	man	z	zebra

*A blend is
a string of
two or three
consonants
which
blend together
yet retain their
original sounds.*

Blends

A blend is a string of two or three consonants (bl, str) which blend together yet retain their original sounds.

Initial Blends

The blends with **l**	bl	cl		fl	gl	pl		
The blends with **r**	br	cr	dr	fr	gr	pr	tr	
The blends with **w**			dw				tw	
The blends with **s**	sc	sp	st	sk	sm	sn	squ	sl	sw
The triple blends	scr	spr	str	spl				
The digraph blends	shr		thr					

Teaching Blends

There are two main options for teaching blends:

• Select a published adult beginner book that includes instruction on blends. Supplement the activities in the book with extra words.

• Develop a file or list of key words to help the student practice and remember the sounds of the blends.

1. Generate a list of words that begin with a selected blend. Any reading selection can be used as a source of words to start the list. Consider words of personal significance to the student.

2. Help the student read the list and isolate the sounds at the beginning of the words.

3. Reread the list with the student, emphasizing the blend.

4. After introducing a sound, provide practice for your student either by following an instructional series or by developing your own exercises.

Digraphs

A digraph is a pair of consonants that forms a new sound. The original sounds of the letters are lost.

CH: Makes a fairly consistent sound. Sometimes the H is silent (echo, mechanic) and sometimes CH sounds like SH (chef, Chicago, pistachio). The CH is silent in the word "yacht."

GH: It can have 3 different sounds:

GH as F: Tough, rough, enough, cough, laugh, slough

GH as G: ghost, spaghetti, ghetto, dinghy, aghast

GH silent: dough, through, eight, caught, straight, night

NG: You cannot hear a true N or G sound. Teach this sound by using word families (-ing, -ang).

NK: A combination of a digraph (NG) and a K sound. The sound is really NGK. Teach this sound by using word families (-ink, -ank).

PH: Has the same sound as F (phone, photograph, physical, alphabet).

SH: A consistent sound that can be sustained.

TH: There are actually two TH sounds:

Unvoiced: Soft and whispered (thank, three, thumb)

Voiced: Buzzy (this, these, they)

Put your fingertips on your throat as you make the sounds to feel the difference or your hands over each ear to hear the difference. Dictionaries distinguish between the two sounds with slightly different symbols.

Most students do not need to know that two TH sounds exist.

WH: While many people pronounce WH the same as W, some people pronounce the WH like an HW, putting a subtle puff of air before the W.

Most students do not need to know that two WH sounds exist.

A digraph is a pair of consonants that forms a new sound.

ch	**sh**	**th**	**ph**
children	shoe	the	photo
check	she	that	phonics
chin	short	this	pharmacy
chest	shut	their	physician
church	shell	these	phrase
cheek	ship	them	
change	shall		
cheer	shirt	three	**wh**
	show	thirty	
ng	shovel	thing	white
	shower	third	where
sing	shout	thumb	what
bring	sharp	thunder	when
wing	sheep	thread	which
ring	shelf	thick	why
wrong	shift	thought	wheel
spring	shin	thank	while
song	shine	Thanksgiving	whether
rang	shimmer	Thursday	whistle

3-D Flashcards

The digraph sounds are sometimes difficult for students to learn. Using three-dimensional flashcards is a good way to help the student remember the sound. They provide an opportunity to utilize the visual, auditory, and kinesthetic/tactile learning styles.

shell

1. Select word to be learned.
2. Print the word on a 5 x 8 flashcard.
3. Glue physical item to flashcard.

   Student utilizes multisensory approach to learn word.

3-D Flashcards can be easily stored in a regular 5 x 8 card file.

VOWEL SOUNDS

There are five vowels: A, E, I, O, U (and sometimes Y and W).

Every word has at least one vowel.

Each vowel has two main sounds: a short sound and a long sound. A vowel should generally be considered short unless there is some sign or signal to tell you it is long.

The vowel sounds are more difficult to learn because:

- They have several different sounds.
- Some sounds are almost alike.
- Sometimes it is difficult to tell which sound to use in a new word.

Each vowel has two main sounds: a short sound and a long sound.

The eighteen vowel sounds in English

5 SHORT	5 LONG
a (apple)	a (ate)
e (echo)	e (eat)
i (in)	i (ice)
o (olive)	o (oats)
u (up)	u (use)

3 R-CONTROLLED	5 OTHER
ar (art)	aw/au (awful)
er/ir/ur (urgent)	oy/oi (oil)
or (or)	ow/ou (out)
	oo (boot)
	oo (book)

SHORT VOWELS

Start with short vowel sounds. Introduce one vowel sound at a time. Provide practice for your student either by following an instructional series or by developing your own exercises using short vowel word families.

The words below may help your student hear the difference between the short vowel sounds.

SHORT a	SHORT e	SHORT i	SHORT o	SHORT u
apple	echo	itch	October	umbrella
answer	end	in	octopus	umpire
ant	exit	is	olive	unlucky
angle	exercise	it	opportunity	ugly
ad	evidence	Indian	operation	uncle
animal	episode	igloo	optical	under
axle	elevator	inch	object	understand
actress	escalator	interception	occupation	us
ask	elephant	infield	octane	up
ashes	egg	injury	opposite	upset

LONG VOWELS

Introduce one vowel sound at a time. Provide practice for your student either by following an instructional series or by developing your own exercises using long vowel word families.

The rules on the following page will help you to determine if the vowel should be long. The list of words following the rules will provide your student with practice in hearing long vowel sounds in words.

In long vowels, the name of the letter and the long vowel sound are the same.

Long Vowel Rules

An E at the end of a word makes the vowel long.

not	note
kit	kite
rod	rode

When two vowels are together, the first vowel is long and the second vowel is silent.

seat	coat	maid
beef	bean	toad
loan	toast	bait

A vowel at the end of a syllable is usually long.

ba/con	go	ba/by
A/pril	e/ven	i/dea
o/pen	o/ver	he/ro

LONG a	LONG e	LONG i	LONG o	LONG u
able	each	idea	open	use
ace	eek	I'll	over	usual
ache	easy	iris	omit	unit
aide	eat	I'm	owe	union
aim	eel	item	oatmeal	uniform
ape	ego	icy	own	unison
apex	ether	Irish	obey	unicorn
ate	east	iodine	Ohio	useless
agency	either	Iowa	oak	universe
alien	even	ideal	odor	ukulele

Other Vowels

- Introduce one new vowel sound at a time.

- Use words that are part of your student's sight word vocabulary as examples.

- The words below may help your student practice these new sounds.

- These vowel combinations are best learned by using word families.

R-Controlled Vowels

ir
girl
girdle
sir
stir

er
her
sister
fern
member

ur
urchin
urge
furniture
murder

ar
farm
arm
are
artist
Arthur

or
or
orbit
orchestra
bore
ornament

oo	oo
book	broom
good	ooze
stood	school
crook	food
shook	boot

al	au	aw
all	auction	awful
always	August	awkward
also	author	awe
call	autumn	lawn
already	automatic	claw

oi	oy
oil	boy
join	oyster
avoid	joyful
coin	boycott
rejoice	enjoy

ou	ow
ouch	how
out	now
our	brown
loud	cow
about	down

Preparation

Before attempting word families, your student must know the consonant sounds and how to rhyme. Most students understand rhyming after being given a few examples. If your student has trouble, do not teach word families yet.

Procedure

1. Select a word family pattern from words your student knows.

    at

2. Write the pattern and ask your student to read it.

    If your student hesitates, say "at."

3. Write a rhyming word underneath. Ask the student for the word. If the student doesn't know the word, supply it.

    at

    mat

4. Keep going.

5. Have the student reread the list.

    at
    mat
    cat
    pat

Variations

- Keep each word family on a separate file card for easy reference and review.

- For extra review, point to words in random order on the list.

- Include nonsense words. (Do not use nonsense words with students learning English as a Second Language.) Explain to your student that some of the words are not real words, but may be part of longer words.

> **mem** is part of   member
> **tem** is part of temperature
> **lem** is part of lemon

- Make flashcards for each family (-ap, -ell, -ot, etc.). Make another set of cards for each consonant, blend, or digraph. Place the consonant cards in front of a family and flip through the letters.

- Get a set of index cards that have a spiral binding and cut the cards as shown below. Use the right hand side for the family and the left hand side for the consonants, blends, and digraphs.

b	an

To help the student understand the meaning of the words generated using word families, use the words in context. For example:

can

> I bought a **can** of coffee.
> I **can** do that.

pop

> Bring me a bottle of **pop** from the store.
> Before the light bulb burned out, there was a loud **pop**.

wave

> The large **wave** crashed on the shore.
> **Wave** to all the people.

Asking for definitions also clarifies the subtle sound differences between such words as PEN and PIN, or BAN and BAND. When your student gives an incorrect definition, use the opportunity to show both spellings and explain the difference.

Word families are also used to:

- Enlarge the student's reading vocabulary.

- Teach spelling skills.

- Prepare the student for using longer words.

- Prepare the student to read independently.

When your student gives an incorrect definition, use the opportunity to show both spellings and explain the difference.

How to Teach Syllables

The use of syllabication is one key that many skilled readers use in unlocking multisyllabic words. It is a skill that will enable new readers to begin to decode more complex material.

Syllables are taught as part of phonics because syllabication affects vowel sounds. Each syllable must have one and only one vowel sound.

Listed below are the basic **traditional** rules.

Rule 1: A consonant between two vowels usually goes with the second vowel unless the first vowel is accented and short.

be/gin   **cab/in**

Rule 2: Consonants between vowels are divided unless they are a blend or digraph.

sil/ver   **pro/phet**

Rule 3: When three consonants are between two vowels, divide between the blend or the digraph and the other consonant.

ar/cher   **tan/trum**

Rule 4: Prefixes always form separate syllables.

dis/close   **pre/pare**

Rule 5: Always divide compound words.

foot/ball   **sea/plane**

Rule 6: Final **le** picks up the preceding consonant to form a syllable.

a/ble   **prin/ci/ple**

The three simple rules below are a combination of the rules on the previous page. You may wish to teach the traditional rules to the more advanced student.

THE TWO-CONSONANT RULE

If there are two consonants between the vowels, divide the word between the consonants.

    in/to   les/son   traf/fic   fen/der

Do not divide blends or digraphs.

    bash/ful   em/blem

THE ONE-CONSONANT RULE

If the word has only one consonant between two vowels, divide the word before the consonant. The vowel is long.
The letter 'y' in the middle or the end of a word acts as a vowel.
The combinations -tion and -sion are one syllable.

la/dy   ba/con   pro/mo/tion   fe/male

THE ONE CONSONANT 'OOPS' RULE:

Sometimes the above rule for one consonant does not work. When that happens, divide the word after the consonant. The vowel is short.

lem/on   vis/it   sec/ond   ov/en   trav/el

The following steps will help in the teaching of three simple syllabication rules.

1. **Mark the vowels (•)**
2. **Cross out final 'e'**
3. **Mark 'r' controlled vowels Δ**
4. **Mark digraphs and blends ~**
5. **Divide the word according to the rules above.**

Divide the following words into syllables.

Example

introducing   in|tro|du|cing

funny   _____

napkin   _____

midnight   _____

compete   _____

pretend   _____

independent   _____

thunderstorm   _____

silverware   _____

vacation   _____

remember   _____

comprehend   _____

inspection   _____

See page 95 for the answers.

Compound Words

A compound word is made by putting words together.

shoe	+	lace	=	shoelace
paper	+	back	=	paperback
work	+	room	=	workroom

Tutors can use compound words to help the student

- Understand the concept of syllabication
  drug / store

- Bridge the gap from single syllable word families to more complex words
  lone   lonesome

- Increase comprehension by using the word(s) within words to extract meaning
  never/the/less

Compound words are found on page 219.

Contractions

Our spoken language blends words and letters together. Contractions are an example. Contractions are two words combined together. An apostrophe substitutes for the missing part.

do + not = don't

Adult new readers use contractions as a natural part of their spoken vocabulary and will see them frequently in print. English as a Second Language students find it difficult to use contractions.

Word lists to study are found on page 230.

A compound word is made by putting words together.

Did you remember all the steps?

1. **Mark the vowels (•)**
2. **Cross out final 'e'**
3. **Mark 'r' controlled vowels △**
4. **Mark digraphs and blends ~**
5. **Divide the word according to the rules.**

funny — fun|ny

napkin — nap|kin

midnight — mid|night

compete — com|pet̶e̶

pretend — pre|tend

independent — in|de|pen|dent

thunderstorm — thun|der|storm

silverware — sil|ver|war̶e̶

vacation — va|ca|tion

remember — re|mem|ber

comprehend — com|pre|hend

inspection — in|spec|tion

See page 93 for the questions

The Zoo

I went to the zoo with John. My sons went too.

We saw lions, tigers, and elephants. We want to go again soon.

A Language Experience Story
by Don

Creating Text

Section 5

CREATING TEXT

Reader + Text + Context = Reading

There is no greater power than being able to put one's thoughts in print.
Writing brings empowerment.

CREATING TEXT

In order to function in today's society, it is necessary to be able to communicate in a written form.

This communication may be:

- a note to a child's teacher
- a job application
- a check
- a grocery list
- a thank you letter

Adults should be able to write in both manuscript and cursive forms, depending upon the type of communication.

Students need to realize the goal for adult penmanship is *legibility*. Each adult develops a personal style of writing. The student is the final judge.

Tips On Penmanship

- Beginning writers should use a pencil. Later exercises can be copied in ink.
- Practice sessions should be limited to 10 minutes. Beginning writers experience fatigue and hand cramps.
- Show the student various samples of penmanship from real life. Let the student select the model to follow.
- Some students find it helpful to trace large examples of the letter to visualize the form.

Practice • Practice • Practice

A a	N n
B b	O o
C c	P p
D d	Q q
E e	R r
F f	S s
G g	T t
H h	U u
I i	V v
J j	W w
K k	X x
L l	Y y
M m	Z z

My name is Don.
I am learning to print.
John is my tutor.
He has very good printing.
It is hard to print small.
I need to write orders at
work.
I practice writing every day.
ol is my hardest letter.
d d d d

May 5, 1989

Aa	*Nn*
Bb	*Oo*
Cc	*Pp*
Dd	*Qq*
Ee	*Rr*
Ff	*Ss*
Gg	*Tt*
Hh	*Uu*
Ii	*Vv*
Jj	*Ww*
Kk	*Xx*
Ll	*Yy*
Mm	*Zz*

I'm Eddie and my
writing is not great!
When I write the letters
don't always go the way I
want. It takes too long to
write neatly. My hand
starts to hurt. Margaret
says I hold my pen too
tightly. I want to be a
waiter. I know I must
learn to write faster and be neat
so the cook can read my orders.

April 12, 1989

My name is Maria and I am learning to write in cursive. It is very frustrating and I get tired quickly. I still need paper with big lines and lots more practice. I am sure that with Cassie's help and patience, some day, I will be able to write just like everybody else and not be embarrassed at work.

June 11, 1989

Spelling is the formation of words from letters according to accepted usage.

Spelling instruction involves two steps:

- The student must recognize the sequence of letters that composes that word.
- The student must have at least a general idea of the meaning of the word.

CONCRETE

Concrete words (objects), may easier to master and they can be selected from Language Experience Stories or from the published materials that your student is using. Adults can learn names of family and friends, words from work, street names, etc... to begin a "bank" of spelling words.

FUNCTION

Function words, such as "what", "this", "is", "for", are harder to master and require more repetition. These words are best practiced in real writing activities. You will find that your student's spelling skills will progress more rapidly if there is a purpose for the writing task.

PRACTICAL APPLICATIONS OF SPELLING

Filling in a calendar, date book, or address book; writing a note to a friend or family member; sending a birthday card; ordering something from a catalog; writing a grocery list; etc... all provide practical ways for your adult student to use spelling words learned and add new words to the student's word bank.

SPELLING NEEDS

The tutor can use the **Spelling** exercise of *Where to Start* to help determine the needs of the student. There are many ways to teach spelling and the following sequence of skills should be adjusted to meet the individual needs of the new writer.

Spelling is the formation of words from letters according to accepted usage.

Spelling Checklist

Beginning Level:

- Writing of initial consonant sounds (page 184)
- Spelling Beginning Sight Words (page 227)
- Spelling Beginning (short vowel) Word Families (page 192)
- Writing personal information (name, address, ...)
- Completing Beginning Guided Writing exercise

Intermediate Level:

- Spelling Intermediate (long vowel) Word Families (page 198)
- Spelling Beginning and Intermediate Word Families using blends and digraphs (page 192 - 207)
- Spelling Intermediate Sight Words (page 227)
- Spelling 100 Most Frequent Words (page 229)
- Adding endings to known words (-s, -ed, -ing)
- Completing Intermediate Guided Writing exercise

Advanced Level:

- Spelling Advanced Word Families (complex vowel combinations) (page 215)
- Spelling Compound Words and Contractions (page 219 - 222)
- Spelling Advanced Sight Words (page 228)
- Adding more complex endings (-tion, -sion, ...) to known words
- Spelling multisyllabic words
- Dictionary skills
- Completing Advanced Guided Writing exercise

The following Strategies can be used to help your student with spelling.

Recorded Spelling

Strategy 21

Rationale: Provides easy, private practice for spelling.

Materials: tape recorder

paper

pencil

Procedure: Tutor tapes a spelling list generated from discussion with student. "What words do you need to learn to spell?"

The tutor records the words using the following format:

1. Say the word.

2. Use the word in a sentence.

3. Say the word again.

4. Pause long enough for the student to write the word (about 15-20 seconds).

5. Record 10 words using this format.

6. Spell each word at the end of the fifth word for a self check.

Strategy 22

Spelling Patterns

Rationale: Use of rhyming words enables the student to use visual and auditory clues for spelling success.

Materials: Lists of word families from **LITSTART** Appendices.

Procedure: Tutor dictates a spelling list derived from word families.

at	**own**	**ight**
bat	down	light
cat	gown	might
hat	town	night
mat	clown	right
pat	drown	sight
sat	frown	tight

Ways to Practice

Strategy 23

Rationale: Incorporates all the senses in learning to spell.

Materials: pencil

paper

Procedure:
1. Tutor says a word.
2. Student says the word.
3. Tutor repeats word and writes it for student to see.
4. Student closes eyes and tries to picture word.
5. Tutor asks student to trace word on the table (allows student to look at the word while tracing it if needed.)
6. Student then writes the word on a piece of paper.
7. Tutor makes corrections as needed and repeats process until mastery.
   (Limit exercise to 10 minutes.)

Strategy 24

3 Steps to Spelling

Rationale: Provides more practice.

Materials: Paper and pencil

Procedure:
1. Tutor writes word to be learned on large sheet of paper.
2. Student traces word.
3. Student covers word and writes it. (Repeat step 2 if necessary.)

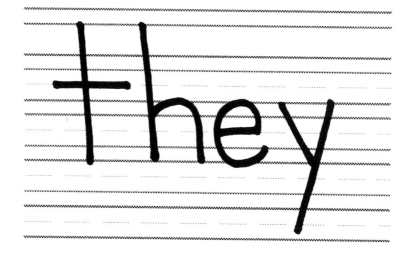

Hangman

Strategy 25

Rationale: Provides a relaxed atmosphere for sustained practice. Students may begin to discover patterns in words and develop strategies they haven't used before.

Materials: Pencil

paper

Procedure:
1. Tutor chooses one of the student's spelling words and draws a blank to represent each letter in the word.

2. The student starts guessing letters to fill in the blanks.

3. For each letter missed the tutor puts a body part on the man.

    If the man is completed before the student guesses the word, the man is hung and the tutor tells the student the word or begins to fill in the blanks so the student can guess.

Hangman is also available on computer software.

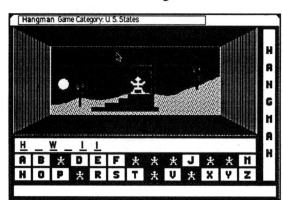

Strategy 26

Cloze Procedure

Rationale: Provides a review for spelling words.
Provides context for spelling words.

Materials: Prepared Lesson Worksheet

Procedure:
1. The tutor prepares a sheet of sentences, each containing a blank where the student can write in the missing spelling word.

2. The student fills in each blank.

3. If the student cannot supply the word based on context, the tutor should say the word.

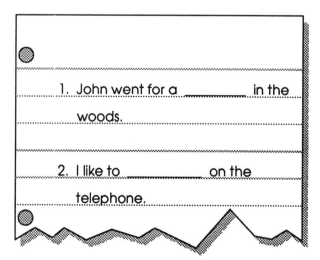

1. John went for a _____ in the woods.

2. I like to _____ on the telephone.

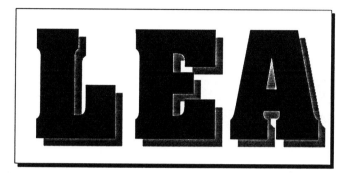

Language Experience Activities (LEAs) are an important part of the tutoring process. They allow the tutor and student:

- to generate and use text containing words that are in the student's oral vocabulary.

- to draw on material familiar to the student.

- to address topics of immediate need to the student.

- to experience immediate success with language.

Language Experience Activities can be used anytime. They provide flexibility and strength to the lesson structure. A faltering lesson can be saved by an LEA.

LEAs can be modified to fit the individual student's needs and interests. LEAs should be used with all students.

Keep a file of the language experience stories written by the student.

- They provide excellent material for future lessons. They can be used for reading, writing, and spelling. One language experience story can be the content for another one.

- They provide a way for the student to measure progress. Part of a lesson can be spent rereading language experience stories. Students are amazed at how fast their reading and writing improve using Language Experience Activities.

Strategy 27

Guided Writing (Beginning)

Rationale: Allows a beginning level student to experience success with writing

Materials: pencil / pen

paper

Procedure:
1. Student supplies topic.
2. Tutor supplies words or phrases to make a word map.

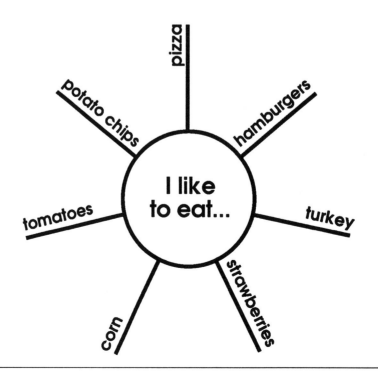

3. The student creates text from the map.

4. The student reads the sentences written.

I like to eat pizza.

I like to eat hamburgers.

I like to eat turkey.

I like to eat strawberries.

I like to eat corn.

I like to eat tomatoes.

I like to eat potato chips.

Strategy 28   *Guided Writing (Intermediate)*

Rationale: Allows the intermediate student to experience success with writing.

Materials: Pencil/pen

paper

Procedure:
1. The tutor picks a word or phrase and writes it in the center of the paper.

2. The student supplies words that come to mind about the topic.

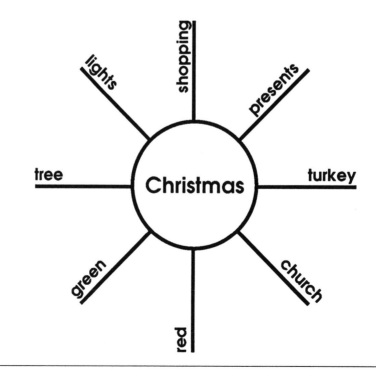

3. The tutor places the words on a word map.

4. The student uses the map to write a story.

5. The student reads the story to the tutor.

At Christmas time my brother and I

like to go shopping for presents. We

trim each tree in our yard with red

and green lights. We buy a turkey

for Christmas dinner. The whole

family goes to church on Christmas.

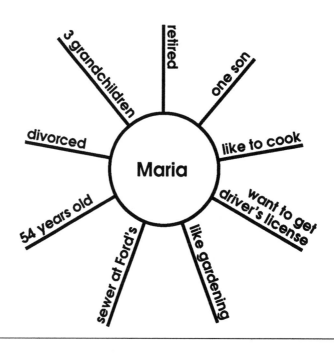

Strategy 29 — *Guided Writing (Advanced)*

Rationale: Provides an oppportunity for an advanced level student to experience success with writing.

Materials: pencil/pen

paper

Procedure:
1. The student supplies a topic.
2. The tutor (or student, if appropriate) prepares a word map.
3. The student uses the map to write a story.
4. The student reads the story.

I'd like to tell you about myself. My name is Maria and I am 54 years old. I worked at a Ford factory and I've just retired. I've been divorced for the last 15 years and have raised a wonderful son all by myself. He is a college graduate and he has a wife and three wonderful children. I love to have them over and cook. My son says I'm the best cook in the world. I also like to grow and can my own vegetables. After I learn to read better, I want to get my driver's license.

Strategy 30

Word Families

Rationale: Extension activity for more practice using the student's own words.

Materials: Index cards

Procedure:
1. Choose words from a story that can be made into word family lists. See the appendices for possible examples.
2. Make word cards for each new word.

Beginning

From Don's story, *"I like to Eat"*

chips　tips　lips　dips　rips

Intermediate

From Eddie's story, *"Christmas"*

tree　bee　see　free　flee

light　right　night　might　tonight

Advanced

From Maria's story, *"Maria"*

like　bike　dislike　strike　spike

cook　book　took　look　shook　mistook

Scrabble

Strategy 31

Rationale: Reinforces spelling and writing skills using a tactile approach.

Materials: Scrabble tiles

Procedure:
1. Student and tutor take turns creating words using tiles.
2. Student and tutor try to create a story using the words generated.

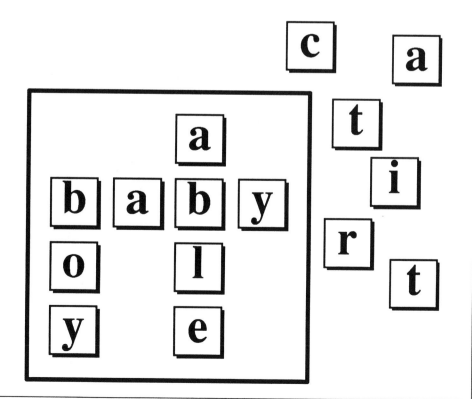

Strategy 32 — Keeping a Journal

Rationale: Shows that writing has a purpose and means communicating thoughts and ideas. Allows tutor and student to get to know each other and provides a record of student progress.

Materials: 2 notebooks (one for the tutor and one for the student)

Procedure:

1. Start with a special question.

   What are you doing for vacation this summer?

2. Tutor and student each keep a separate journal.

3. At each session tutor and student exchange journals and read each other's thoughts and ideas.

   Spelling errors are ignored unless the student is interested in working on specific words.

4. Tutor and student discuss and agree upon a question for next week's entry.

Filling in the Comics

Strategy 33

Rationale: Helps to develop critical thinking and attention to detail, as well as, writing skills.

Materials: Comic strip with dialogue whited out.

Procedure: Tutor helps student write in the missing dialogue.

CRANKSHAFT   **By Tom Batiuk and Chuck Ayers**

Strategy 34 — **Mixed-up Cartoons**

Rationale: Aids in sequencing of events and developing prediction strategies. Aids in structuring a story.

Materials: Cartoon
Scissors

Procedure:
1. Tutor cuts the cartoon into separate boxes.
2. Tutor asks student to put the boxes in the right order.
3. Tutor and student discuss the sequence and possible story ideas.

CRANKSHAFT   **By Tom Batiuk and Chuck Ayers**

Written Conversation

Strategy 35

Rationale: Provides additional writing practice for the purpose of communicating thoughts and ideas.

Materials: Pencil
Paper

Procedure:
1. Tutor write a question.
2. Student writes the answer. Ignore spelling errors.
3. Tutor keeps asking questions-passing the note back and forth. The challenge is to conduct this exercise with a minimum of conversation.

Strategy 36

Rationale: _____
_____
_____
_____
_____

Materials: _____
_____
_____
_____

Procedure: 1. _____
_____
2. _____
_____
3. _____
_____

Strategy 37

Rationale: _____

_____

_____

_____

_____

Materials: _____

_____

_____

_____

Procedure: 1. _____

_____

2. _____

_____

3. _____

_____

The best theories are useless without a proper plan of action.

The Tutoring Experience

Section 6

THE TUTORING EXPERIENCE

Reader + Text + Context = Reading

*The **tutor** is the catalyst in the reading process.*

THE TUTORING EXPERIENCE

Welcome

Welcome to the world of tutoring! Thank you for caring.

You are needed. Twenty percent of the adults in the United States are functionally illiterate, which means they cannot read well enough to function independently in modern society.

The solution to the problems of illiteracy lies in partnerships. Partnerships between national, state, and local agencies as well as volunteers from your own community provide the financial, material, and people resources to combat illiteracy.

As a tutor you will be establishing a partnership with a new reader. This section of LITSTART will provide you with strategies and support to make this a successful partnership.

You are joining a network of volunteers that spans from coast to coast fighting illiteracy. Enjoy your adventure with your student!

> *The successful tutor
> is someone
> who cares.*

Meet John, Margaret, and Cassandra

Tutors, like students, come from diverse backgrounds, diverse educational experiences, and with many different reasons for wanting to be reading tutors. John, Margaret and Cassandra are typical of the thousands of tutors across the United States helping someone learn to read.

Many tutors find they are getting back as much as they are giving.

John: Don's Tutor

**"Don has really become a good friend.
We have shared so many things together.
He is like the son I never had..."**

John is a retired veterinarian who enjoys fishing and wildlife photography. John learned about the literacy program from a poster in his local library. After taking the tutor training, John was assigned to work with Don, a student in adult education. He has been working with Don for the past one and a half years and they enjoy sharing stories about animals. John helped Don get his library card, and he also took Don and his two sons on a guided tour of the zoo.

John has made several trips to Africa to photograph wild animals.

Margaret: Eddie's Tutor

**"Working with Eddie has been
one of the most rewarding
experiences in my life..."**

Margaret is close to retirement. She is a waitress and has worked
in the same restaurant for the last 25 years. Her student, Eddie, is
a dishwasher in the same restaurant. When Eddie had a chance to
move from dishwasher to waiter, he confided in Margaret that he
couldn't read. Margaret had heard about the literacy program on
television. She and Eddie made the phone call together to ask for
more information.

She enjoys cooking and likes reading Agatha Christie novels.

Cassandra: Maria's Tutor

**"I saw my mom's excitement when her student
learned to read..."**

Cassie heard about the literacy program from her mother who has been
a volunteer tutor for the last two years.

Cassie is a first grade teacher in an inner city school. She is unmarried
and living with her parents. Cassie decided to become a volunteer
tutor when she realized that many of the parents of her students could
not read well enough to help with their school work. Cassie and Maria
have worked together for the last six months. They meet at Cassie's
school after the children have left for the day. Maria has chosen many
books from Cassie's school library to read to her grandchildren.

Your initial contact with your student will usually be over the telephone to make arrangements for your weekly tutoring session.

When your student answers:

1. Introduce yourself. Ask if this is a good time to talk.

2. Tell the student you are looking forward to working together. Explain that at the first meeting you will talk about the student's particular needs and answer any questions.

3. Select a day and a time that is convenient for both of you.

4. Select a location that is quiet and on neutral ground (library, church, community center, school, college, or business). Small private rooms are best. Avoid meeting in your student's home or your home.

5. Give your student your telephone number, slowly. Ask the student to call if there will be a problem making the session.

If your student is not at home:

Simply leave your name and telephone number. (Sometimes the student's family does not know about the student's reading problem.)

If you need assistance in arranging for a tutoring site, contact your local literacy organization.

FIRST MEETING: OBJECTIVES

Primary Objective:

To encourage and reassure your student about the decision to improve reading.

Possible things to say:

"I'm here to help you learn what you WANT to learn."

"Don't worry about mistakes. Mistakes help us learn."

"Please ask questions."

Secondary Objective:

To learn about your student.

You will be most effective as a tutor if you know what your student's goals, needs, interests, and abilities are. This information will help you plan your weekly lessons.

OUTLINE FOR FIRST MEETING

Materials and Supplies

LITSTART
Lined paper
Pencils, pens, eraser, highlighter
Pocket dictionary
Small cards for experience story (optional)
Carbon paper (optional)
Published materials (Laubach, LVA, others)

Introduction

Smile and introduce yourself.
Make sure you are pronouncing and spelling the student's name correctly.
Explain your purpose. Discuss the student's needs and answer any questions.

Personal Information

Chat with your student. Get to know your student as an individual. Be interested in the student's life and goals, but do not probe.

Questions you might ask are:

How far did you go in school?
Did you like school?
Do you ever read any signs, ads, books, or mail?
What type of work do you do?
Do you have to do any reading or writing at your job?
What would you like to learn?
What is your goal?
What do you do in your spare time?

Reading Ability

Do the *Where to Start* exercise (unless you have other information about your student's ability).

Spelling Ability (optional)

If your student would like to try some spelling, use the *Where to Start* Spelling exercise.

Experience Story

If time permits, the language experience activity is an excellent icebreaker. This exercise is optional for the first meeting. You may want to use it with an intermediate or advanced student on the first meeting.

Conclusion

- Summarize your findings and what you will try for the next lesson.
- Confirm the time, date, and place of your next meeting.
- Ask the student for questions or suggestions.
- PRAISE the student!

PREPARING FOR THE 2nd MEETING

In your first meeting you gathered information about your student's personal background, interests, and goals. You also determined whether the student is reading on the beginning, intermediate, or advanced level.

Your goal is to find materials and activities that will be appealing to your student and help reach the student's goals. This section will focus on how to organize this information into weekly lesson plans.

Selecting Materials

Finding the right reading material for your student is a major key to success. A fascinating, well-written, attractive book can increase progress, inspire new goals, and excite your student about the whole learning process.

Make the student's goal the immediate focus of your lessons. Get the exact materials your student wants to work on such as labels, checks, books, catalogs, etc.

No one can predict which materials will work best for you and your student. Experiment. Get feedback from your student. Try again. The best selection may be a combination of materials. Choose a variety of materials and give the student a choice.

There are 4 things to consider when choosing materials.

1. Subject matter .... Related to student's goals and interests.

2. Reading level .... Written at student's level.

3. Skills .... Covers the skills your student needs.

4. Appearance .... Utilizes pictures, white space, print size.

Local Literacy Organization

Ask your literacy coordinator for policies on borrowing or buying books.

Public Library's Adult Basic Reading Collection

Take your student to the library and encourage the student to get a library card.

Adult Basic Education (ABE) Program

Call your local literacy coordinator, community education office, or school administration for policies on borrowing or buying books.

Experience Story

This strategy can generate a wealth of reading material based on the student's own life and interests.

Material Publishers

You can order some materials yourself. A listing of publishers can be found in the Appendices.

Yourself

Try writing a selection geared to your student's interests and vocabulary.

Student's Home

Encourage your student to bring mail or other reading matter from home or work.

Children's Books

Do not use such books unless your student wants to practice reading to children.

Some books written for older children are acceptable to adults. This includes books about history, culture, celebrities, or science. Screen all books carefully; make sure the book does not talk down to the reader or use juvenile pictures.

Everyday Reading Materials

The reading materials below are readily available, inexpensive, and may relate to your student's goal.

Advertisements
    Department stores
    Grocery stores
    Others

Bills

Boxes
    Cereal
    Other foods
    Detergent

Bumper stickers

Bus schedules

Calendars

Catalogs
    Adult education classes
    Gift stores
    Specialties

Containers

Cookbooks

Coupons

Forms
    Credit application
    Job application
    Insurance
    Income tax
    Registration

Greeting cards

Identification

Instruction books
    Appliances
    Equipment for job
    Games
    Vehicles

Labels
    Cleaning products
    Clothing
    Food packages
    Medicine bottles
    Toiletries
    Records

Magazines

Mail

Maps

Membership cards

Menus

Newsletters

Newspaper Articles
    Advice columns
    Comics
    Movie ads
    Recipes
    Sports
    Store ads
    Want ads
    Weather

Notes from school

Packages
    Frozen food

Programs
    Plays
    Sports events

Price tags

Recipes

Report cards

Song lyrics

Street signs

Telephone book

Text books

TV magazine

Vending machine instructions

Wrappers

Preparing A Lesson Plan

The weekly Lesson Plan is an annotated outline listing the specific topics that you intend to cover.

The length of your lesson will depend on your student. An hour is the limit of concentration for some students; others can handle two hours or more if they get a break and a variety of activities. Experiment. You and your student may decide to meet more than just once weekly. That will require additional planning.

The typical Lesson Plan contains three parts:

1. Reading

2. Keys

3. Creating Text

Lesson Plan for Meeting # _____

Prep Time: _____
Tutor Time: _____
Total Time
For Lesson: _____

Name _____ Date _____

MATERIALS (titles / pages) _____
_____
_____
_____
_____

READING

Pre-Reading _____
_____
_____

KEYS • Phonics • Word Families • Sight Words
_____
_____
_____

CREATING TEXT - WRITING
_____
_____
_____
_____

Back-up Plans _____
_____
_____

Extra Work _____
_____
_____

Ideas for Next Lesson _____
_____
_____

Outline for Preparing a Lesson

1. Review your materials.

2. Using a blank Lesson Plan form, start with the **Reading** part of the lesson. Write down the titles or page numbers you will cover. (See Section 3.)

3. Read the material to be covered. Think about activities you can use before, during, and after the reading. Make notes about specific words, concepts, or questions on the Lesson Plan form.

4. Think about the **Keys** part of your lesson. Select or modify activities from a book or design your own. On the Lesson Plan form, list specific letters, words, word families, pages, topics, sentences, or exercises. (See Section 4.)

5. Think about the **Creating Text** part of your lesson. Select or modify activities from a book or design your own. List specific items to be covered on the Lesson Plan form. (See Section 5.)

6. If you are using new materials or new activities, make a note on your Lesson Plan form to preview the materials with your student and to get feedback after the exercise.

7. Think about things your student could do at home between sessions. Make notes on the bottom of your Lesson Plan.

8. Review your lesson plan. If there are any topics you are unsure of, review them.

9. Have a back-up plan ready if materials are too difficult for the student.

It is wise, at first, to prepare more material than you expect to cover; better too much than not enough. Also, until you have a thorough understanding of your student's abilities, it is better to design a lesson that is too easy rather than too difficult.

Don

Lesson Plan for Meeting # 5

Name _Don_   Date _3/5/88_

Prep Time:	_1 hour_
Tutor Time:	_2½ hrs._
Total Time For Lesson:	_3.5 hrs._

MATERIALS (titles / pages) _Language Experience Story — "I like to eat..."_
Word Cards
Focus on Phonics I   "P" + "T"   "p" on page 8
"t" on page 14

READING

Pre-Reading ① _Discuss other foods Don likes to eat._
② _Make new word cards._
③ _Start discussion about work._
④ _New LEA story — "Pets I sell are..."_

KEYS • Phonics • Word Families • Sight Words
Beginning sounds /p/ + /t/
Word family -ip (chips)
Sight words: pizza, prepare, python

CREATING TEXT - WRITING
① _Rewrite expanded LEA story with new foods._
② _Write new sight words for word file._
③ _Write new word family words._

Back-up Plans _Practice name and address form._
Write new experience story on pets

Extra Work _Find words in the newspaper that_
begin with "p" and "t"

Ideas for Next Lesson _Have Don bring a feed order form_
for the pet store. Ask Don if he uses
an animal catalog to choose animals to buy.
Use it to do Guided Writing exercise.

John

Lesson Plan for Meeting # 10

Name _Eddie_   Date _4-6-89_

Prep Time:	45 min.
Tutor Time:	2 hours
Total Time For Lesson:	2¾ hrs.

MATERIALS (titles / pages) _Challenger 1 – Lesson 8_
"At the Amusement Park" pp. 28-33
Focus on Phonics 3 – p. 10 (-ake)
p. 47 (-oke)
Menu from Jones Bar & Grill

READING

Pre-Reading _Talk about an amusement park: if Eddie had a friend who had never been to a park, what would he want to tell him about it? Use story mapping strategy to identify vocabulary and make predictions about story. Read story._

KEYS • Phonics • Word Families • Sight Words
Using -ake or -oke lists in Challenger, have Eddie make new rhyming words to be used for spelling activity. Let Eddie select 5 words from his menu to learn and practice.

CREATING TEXT - WRITING _Discuss activity on p 33 (writing sentences). Do half of them together (Eddie does rest for homework). Practice writing orders from menu._

**Eddie**

Back-up Plans _Create an LEA from story map. Select a book from library on a rock singer or group Eddie's interested in._

Extra Work _Eddie does exercises 1, 3, 4 (p. 30, 32) at home from Challenger. If he has time, send Focus on Phonics 3 home & do p. 10 & p. 47._

Ideas for Next Lesson _Work on writing and reading addresses. Eddie brings address book and telephone directory for writing activity._

**Margaret**

Maria

Cassandra

Lesson Plan for Meeting # 2

Prep Time:	30 MIN
Tutor Time:	1½ HR.
Total Time For Lesson:	2 HR.

Name __MARIA__   Date __JUNE 10, 89__

MATERIALS (titles / pages) __LAUBACH SKILLBOOK 4 (LESSON 1)__
"THE COMPUTER AGE"

DRIVER'S HANDBOOK

LIBRARY CARD APPLICATION

READING

Pre-Reading __USE "LET'S FIND OUT" Strategy BEFORE READING COMPUTER STORY__

USE SQ4R STRATEGY FOR 1ST CHAPTER OF DRIVER'S BOOK — DISCUSS PURPOSE FOR STRATEGY

KEYS • Phonics • Word Families • Sight Words
- DISCUSS ENDINGS FROM P. 7 (SB 4)
- WORK ON COMPOUND WORDS ON P. 6 (USE RAIL/ROAD, STOP/LIGHT, HIGH/WAY AS EXAMPLES)
- CHOOSE LONG Ū WORDS FROM APPENDIX FOR SPELLING WORDS.

CREATING TEXT - WRITING
- EXAMINE LIBRARY CARD APPLICATION TO MAKE SURE MARIA CAN DO IT — HAVE HER FILL IT OUT.
- START LEA STORY ON MARIA'S LIFE. USE MAPPING STRATEGY.

Back-up Plans __STUDY A LOCAL MAP AND HAVE MARIA IDENTIFY STREETS SHE KNOWS. PICK OUT BOOKS FOR MARIA TO READ TO HER GRANDCHILDREN — INDEPENDENT LEVEL.__

Extra Work __PRACTICE PRINTING FORM ON P. 5 (SB4) DO ADDITIONAL EXERCISES ON P. 6 + 7 (CHECK NEXT TIME).__

Ideas for Next Lesson __HAVE MARIA BRING A BOOK FOR SUSTAINED SILENT READING. REVIEW NEW DRIVING TERMS. BRING IN MORE COMPUTER ARTICLES TO ANSWER GENERATED QUESTIONS.__

Lesson Plan for Meeting # _____

Name _____ Date _____

Prep Time: _____
Tutor Time: _____
Total Time
For Lesson: _____

MATERIALS (titles / pages) _____
_____
_____
_____
_____
_____
_____

READING

Pre-Reading _____
_____
_____
_____
_____

KEYS • Phonics • Word Families • Sight Words
_____
_____
_____
_____
_____
_____

CREATING TEXT - WRITING
_____
_____
_____
_____
_____
_____

Back-up Plans _____
_____
_____
_____

Extra Work _____
_____
_____
_____

Ideas for Next Lesson _____
_____
_____
_____

Your first few meetings will involve much preparation and experimentation. Each lesson will provide you with more data which you can use to make the next lesson even better. Revise your routine as you discover materials and activities that work for you and your student.

If an idea worked, use it again. If it didn't, don't use it. Involve your student in the decision process. As you develop a routine of activities that work for your student, the preparation will take less time. In the beginning, though, it pays to spend the time to prepare thoroughly.

If the student would like to do extra practice or independent work at home, have the student:

- Reread a story
- Read a new story (not too difficult)
- Read with a family member, if appropriate
- Review a list of words that you have practiced together
- Answer written questions about a story that was read
- Do workbook exercises
- Practice penmanship
- Practice spelling words
- Copy words or sentences
- Write in a journal
- Listen to tapes of sounds, words, or a reading

At some point your routine may need to be modified. Your student will either finish the book(s), master the skills, or achieve identified goals, or perhaps you will both be ready for a change. You may wish to evaluate goals, find new materials, or experiment with new activities.

This is a good time to stop, evaluate the student's progress, and officially recognize achievements. Give your student a certificate.

CERTIFICATE
OF
ACHIEVEMENT

Presented to

_____

for the following achievement

_____

Congratulations and best wishes
for continued success

Presented by: _____   *Date:* _____

Formal evaluation is beyond the scope of this book, but you can conduct informal evaluations every few months. A Progress Check, similar to the *Where to Start,* is available for this purpose. Your student needs to see progress in order to maintain motivation at a high level.

When your student reaches a goal, it is a time to rejoice. You and your student are to be congratulated on an outstanding job. Acknowledge this progress with a Certificate of Achievement.

Encourage your student to set new goals. Ask your student, "Is there another goal you would like to reach?"

If you both want to continue together, proceed.

If a new goal involves adult education or specialized course work, you may want to offer your assistance.

Notify your literacy coordinator of the student's progress and whether or not you will continue to work together.

CERTIFICATE

OF

ACHIEVEMENT

Presented to

Don Ross

for the following achievement

Voted for the First Time

Congratulations and best wishes

for continued success

Presented by: *John Martin*

Date: **June 23, 1988**

Sit beside your student or around the corner of a table; work together.

If you are right-handed, sit on the right when you write or point. However, when the student writes (if right-handed), sit on the left. This gives you both a clear view. If you or your student is left-handed, do the opposite.

Praise; praise; praise! This is a key tutor responsibility. Even routine work should be constantly acknowledged with a "good" or a nod of the head.

Tell your student not to worry about mistakes. Mistakes are helpful; they tell you what to work on. Mistakes are a good way to learn.

When the student makes an error, say "That's close" or "That's a tricky one" or "Try again," rather than "no" or "That's wrong."

When your student misses words, put the blame where it belongs...on the language. Remind the student that English often violates its own rules.

If YOU make a mistake, say so; let your student see that it is okay to make mistakes. If you don't know an answer, say so. Research the answer later if you can.

Strive for 80%-90% success for your student. This means your student is mastering the material being covered. Below this level, the student may experience frustration.

Watch your student's face. If you detect puzzlement, reteach; if you see frustration, change activities; if you see enlightenment, rejoice with the student; if you see pride, build on it.

If you have an idea for your lesson, do what good tutors do: **Try it!** If it works, do it again. If it doesn't work, don't do it again.

Superb.

This is a winner!

Outstanding!

Very fine work.

You're on the mark.

A splendid job.

Clear, concise, and complete!

I like your style.

It looks like you've put a lot of work into this.

You've shown a lot of patience with this.

I like how you tackled this.

This is quite an accomplishment.

You're on the right track now.

How impressive!

I like the way you've handled this.

Marvelous.

Excellent work.

You've got it now.

You're on target now.

That's the right answer.

Beautiful.

That's right. Good for you.

Nice going.

Congratulations.

That's a good point.

You really outdid yourself today.

What neat work.

I knew you could do it!!

Great going!

That's it!

You're really moving.

Topnotch work.

I appreciate your help.

You make it look so easy.

You're becoming an expert at this.

You've come a long way with this one.

Terrific.

I knew you could do it.

I like the way you are working.

Fantastic! Keep up the good work.

Not sure of what to do?
Lesson not going well?

Don't worry. Relax. Help is here.

Follow these seven steps for a
successful lesson.

1. SMILE.

2. HELP THE STUDENT FIND
   SOMETHING TO READ THAT
   IS OF INTEREST.

3. HAVE THE STUDENT START
   READING ALOUD.

4. TELL THE STUDENT ANY
   UNKNOWN WORDS.

5. ASK QUESTIONS ABOUT THE
   CONTENT.

6. SAY "GOOD."

7. KEEP GOING.

If you experience continued problems, talk to your literacy coordinator
and ask for suggestions.

If you are tutoring independently, reread the tutoring section of this book
for possible remedies.

Section 7

Where to Start

Reader + Text + Context = Reading

Developing a Plan of Action is the first step in achieving success in reading.

Where to Start

The successful tutor needs a Plan of Action. The *Where to Start* Placement Guide is the first step in the Plan of Action. The Guide and Plan are necessary for placement, planning, and progress.

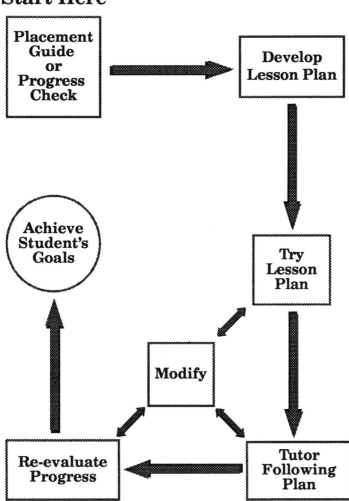

LITSTART

Where to Start

Placement Guide
for

_____

Name   **Date**

Michigan Literacy, Inc.
c/o Library of Michigan
717 W. Allegan
Lansing, MI 48909
(517) 373-4451

Where to Start is designed to help you and your student make some decisions about the student's interests and reading level in order to maximize the effectiveness of the lesson. *Where to Start* consists of five components:

- **Informal Interview**
- **Reading Passages**
- **Writing**
- **Spelling**
- **Letter Identification**

The following pages will provide you with the necessary instructions for using the *Where to Start* Placement Guide (yellow).

The Progress Check (blue) is to be used for checking progress. It is available as a separate document.

Informal Interview

1. What things are you comfortable reading now?

2. Do you read or write at work?   At home?
   With your children?

3. When you get stuck on a word when reading, what do you do?

4. What are your hobbies or special interests?

5. What are you good at?

6. What do you want to learn how to read?

7. What do you need to learn to read and write?

The answers to these questions may give you an idea of the student's reading level. It will help you select materials appropriate to the student's interests and experience. These questions asked later could show a change in your student's reading habits as your lessons progress.

Passage 1

Ten Dollars!

After each reading, check the student's comprehension by asking what is remembered of the passage. Ask additional questions if appropriate.

Tim has a new car.
It is blue and white.
He drives it to work.
It uses a lot of gas.
Tim buys gas each week.
He needs ten dollars for gas.

If your student can read this passage with little or no problem and remembers key ideas, go on to Passage 2.
If your student had difficulty with the passage, the student is at the beginning level. You may wish to do the **Letter Identification** exercise in *Where to Start.*

Passage 2

At the Beach

What do you do in the summer?
I like to go to the beach and enjoy the sun.
Last summer I learned how to wind surf.
I spent many days on the water,
surfing with my friends.
That is how I got so badly sunburned.
This year I will be more careful.

If your student can read this passage with little or no problem and remembers key ideas, go on to Passage 3.
If your student had difficulty with the passage, the student is at the beginning to intermediate level. Proceed to the **Writing** exercise.

Passage 3

Moving Ahead.

John was so excited. He was to be in the company's new computer training program. The company would be training six employees. He was number three on the list. John made sure that he would be successful. He spent his lunch hour, each day, studying the long list of computer words. John decided that there was no way he was going to fail. He had worked hard to get this chance.

If your student can read this story with little or no problem and remembers key ideas, go on to Passage 4.
If your student had difficulty with the passage, the student is at the intermediate level. Proceed to the **Writing** exercise.

Passage 4

The Big Fire

Denise could hear the sirens on the fire trucks as she raced out of her apartment building. Smoke was billowing out of the windows of the big, yellow house across the street. The firemen were connecting the hoses to the fire hydrant. All of a sudden, water began to shoot out of the nozzle on the end of the hose. As the water struck the house, black smoke filled the sky. The fire marshal warned everyone to stand back. Soon the fire was extinguished. All that was left of the house was a pile of debris.

If your student had difficulty with the passage, the student is at the intermediate to advanced level.

If the student had no difficulty with the passage, the student is probably at the advanced level. Proceed to the **Writing** exercise. You will want to do the **Spelling** exercise with the advanced student during the first session.

Writing

Sign your name here _____

Please complete the following form:

Name _____

Address _____

City _____ State _____ Zip Code _____

Spelling

1. _____	11. _____	21. _____	31. _____
2. _____	12. _____	22. _____	32. _____
3. _____	13. _____	23. _____	33. _____
4. _____	14. _____	24. _____	34. _____
5. _____	15. _____	25. _____	35. _____
6. _____	16. _____	26. _____	36. _____
7. _____	17. _____	27. _____	37. _____
8. _____	18. _____	28. _____	38. _____
9. _____	19. _____	29. _____	39. _____
10. _____	20. _____	30. _____	40. _____

Have your student fill out the form above. Provide assistance as needed. If the student had difficulty with the form, do not use the **Spelling** exercise. The **Spelling** exercise is optional for the first meeting. Use of it depends on the individual student. If your student is a very beginning student, the **Spelling** exercise should not be used.

ABC

This exercise is designed to help you determine your student's spelling needs.

- Pronounce each word clearly.
- Give the word in a sentence.
- Repeat the word.
- Have the student write the word.

STOP when your student misses three words in a row or becomes frustrated.

1.	cat	A cat makes a nice pet.	cat
2.	man	The man is smiling.	man
3.	ten	I have ten fingers.	ten
4.	mop	Please mop the floor.	mop
5.	fit	It is important to keep fit.	fit
6.	chin	The ball hit me on the chin.	chin
7.	will	What time will you arrive?	will
8.	pick	Pick up my suit from the cleaners.	pick
9.	tax	How much is the sales tax?	tax
10.	cash	Can you cash my check?	cash
11.	band	My son plays in the band.	band
12.	pump	I need to pump some gas.	pump
13.	still	John is still here.	still
14.	think	What do you think about that?	think
15.	lunch	I had a sandwich for lunch.	lunch

16. cake	I ate the chocolate cake.	cake
17. like	Do you like ice cream?	like
18. feel	I feel a little dizzy.	feel
19. coat	Do not forget to wear your coat.	coat
20. teach	Can you teach me to ice skate?	teach
21. plate	Hand me a plate.	plate
22. grow	Did you grow these tomatoes?	grow
23. clean	On Saturday I clean the house.	clean
24. toast	I like toast and jelly.	toast
25. flight	What time does your flight leave?	flight
26. farm	My mother grew up on a farm.	farm
27. girl	Who is the girl with blonde hair?	girl
28. turn	Make a left turn at the next corner.	turn
29. her	Give her the book.	her
30. third	I play third base on my baseball team.	third
31. spoon	Hand me the wooden spoon.	spoon
32. ground	I fell on the ground.	ground
33. spoil	Candy will spoil your dinner.	spoil
34. caught	I caught a big fish.	caught
35. shook	The wind shook the house.	shook
36. needed	John needed a new pair of shoes.	needed
37. running	Who is running across the field?	running
38. glasses	Please put four glasses on the table.	glasses
39. clapped	The baby clapped her hands.	clapped
40. shaving	My brother is in the bathroom shaving.	shaving

Types of Words

1 - 10 Short vowel words (**B/I**)

11 - 15 Short vowel words ending with blends (**I**)

16 - 20 Long vowel words (**I**)

21 - 25 Long vowel words with blends (**I/A**)

26 - 30 Words with R-controlled vowels (**I**)

31 - 35 Words with other vowels (**A**)

36 - 40 Endings (**I/A**)

B=Beginning **I**=Intermediate **A**=Advanced

Letter Identification

p	b	s	z
t	d	f	v
m	n	g	k
j	c	w	h
r	l	y	x
qu	sh	ch	th

a	e	i	o	u

If your student is at the beginning level, ask the student to tell you the names of the letters. Start at the top and go across each row. Circle all the letters that the student identifies correctly. If the student is able to identify all the letters, you may wish to have the student try to give you the sounds of the letters.

Tips for the Placement Guide & Progress Check

- As the student responds, give frequent praise.

- When the student starts to read haltingly or make mistakes, provide the answer.

> **You have determined the starting level.**

- If you are undecided about which of two levels to use for your student, use the lower level. It is better to start with easier materials and let the student experience success than to start too high.

- Thank the student and explain your findings. " This was very helpful. It gives me an idea of some good books we can use for our next sessions."

- If you have other test information on your student, you may still use *Where to Start* for additional information.

Once you have determined a level for your student, you are ready to begin formulating lesson plans for your student.

Don's *Where to Start* Placement Results

Interview:

Don's tutor, John, learned that Don read almost nothing. He was very embarrassed reading orally. Don was interested in reading his mail and learning to write checks. He would like to get his own checking account. Don has some things at work he would like to be able to read too.

Don loves animals, particularly dogs. He has a German shepherd. Don makes cabinets and tables in his spare time. He likes to hike and fish.

Reading:

Don could not read the first story "Ten Dollars!", but was able to pick out the words car, gas, and work.

In Letter Identification, Don was able to identify all of the letters.

Writing and Spelling:

Don copied his address from his driver's license to fill out the form. John felt it was not necessary to do the spelling exercise at this time.

Conclusion:

John felt that Don needed to start with beginning materials.

Eddie's *Where to Start* Placement Results

Interview:

Margaret, Eddie's tutor, discovered that Eddie could read menus in the restaurant where he worked and some of his mail. Eddie finds reading to be frustrating and he reads only when he absolutely has to. When he gets stuck, Eddie will skip the word or try to figure it out from the rest of the sentence.

Eddie hopes to become a waiter at the restaurant and be able to read and write messages at work. He would also like to take the written test for his driver's license. He likes bowling and watching TV. He also plays the guitar at his church.

Reading:

Eddie had his initial reading assessment done in the literacy office by the reading specialist. The report Margaret received stated that Eddie was reading at the intermediate level. Margaret will use the reading passages as a progress check.

Writing and Spelling:

Margaret skipped Letter Identification . On the Writing exercise, Eddie was able to fill out the form without help. He missed *feel*, *plate*, and *toast* on the Spelling exercise. Margaret noticed he mixed his capital and small letters when printing.

Conclusion:

Margaret and Eddie spent their first lesson looking at the materials sent by the literacy office. They decided to use a menu, from the restaurant where Eddie worked, as supplemental material.

Maria's *Where to Start* Placement Results

Interview:

Cassandra found out that Maria does the word search puzzle and tries to read other parts of the newspaper. She has particular difficulty with big words which upsets her. Reading people's names is difficult for her. She has some trouble remembering what she reads. She would like to read to her grandchildren more, if the books weren't so hard.

Maria's favorite things are gardening, cooking, and travel. She hopes to travel more when she retires. Maps are a problem. Maria's goal is to become more independent.

Reading:

Maria read the first two stories quickly and was able to recall almost all the details. In "Moving Ahead" she started having problems. She missed two words and her fluency was poor. After slowly reading "The Big Fire" and missing three words, Maria was still able to recall much about the story.

Writing and Spelling:

Maria filled out the form with care and 'lovely printing'. On the Spelling exercise, Cassandra stopped after Maria missed *flight, ground,* and *spoil.*

Conclusion:

Cassandra felt that Maria could use some help with intermediate spelling skills, but she was ready to read on an advanced level.

Checklist of Reading and Writing Skills
Beginning Level

❑ Can identify the letters of the alphabet, capital or small, in Appendix P, at random.

❑ Can read words from the **Beginning Word Families List** in Appendix D.

❑ Can read words from the **Beginning Sight Word List** in Appendix K.

❑ Can read the **100 Most Frequent Words in English** in Appendix L.

❑ Can read beginning level material with comprehension.

❑ Can legibly print the alphabet in sequence, both capital and small letters.

❑ Can identify the initial consonant sounds of most words in Appendix A.

❑ Can print personal information on a form and complete a Beginning Guided Writing exercise.

The skills above reflect the minimal skills needed to move to the intermediate level.

Checklist of Reading and Writing Skills
Intermediate Level

❏ Can identify the long and short vowel sounds in beginning and intermediate words.

❏ Can recognize blends and digraphs in Appendices B and C.

❏ Can recognize and divide simple compound words from Appendix H.

❏ Can read and spell words from the **Beginning and Intermediate Word Families Lists** in Appendices D and E.

❏ Can read words from the **Intermediate Sight Word List** in Appendix K.

❏ Can spell and write the **100 Most Frequent Words in English** in Appendix L.

❏ Can read intermediate level material with comprehension.

❏ Can legibly write *in cursive.*

❏ Recognizes and uses the common endings:
-s, -es, -'s, -ed, -ing.

❏ Can complete an Intermediate Guided Writing exercise.

The skills above reflect the minimal skills needed to move to the advanced level.

Checklist of Reading and Writing Skills
Advanced Level

❑ Can identify irregular vowel sounds from the **Advanced Word Families List** in Appendix G.

❑ Can apply rules of syllabication to the words in Appendix J.

❑ Can read and write most compound words and contractions in Appendix H.

❑ Can read and spell words from the **Intermediate and Advanced Word Families Lists** in Appendices E, F, and G.

❑ Can read words from the **Advanced Sight Word List** in Appendix K.

❑ Can use the **100 Most Frequent Words in English** in Appendix L in daily writing.

❑ Can read advanced level material with comprehension.

❑ Uses legible penmanship to complete everyday writing tasks.

❑ Recognizes and uses more complex prefixes and endings: un-, dis-, pre-, -er, -est, -tion, -sion, -ly, and others.

❑ Can complete an Advanced Guided Writing exercise.

❑ Recognizes and uses common contractions in Appendix M.

The skills above reflect the minimal skills needed at the advanced level.

The Appendices

Ready Reference of Resource Materials

Section 8

APPENDICES

Literacy Resources for Tutors

THE APPENDICES

B b

bat
baseball
beer
book
Bible
boy
baby
bottle
bowling
basketball
boxing
birthday
bird
bills
beef

C c

cat
coffee
car
Coke
curve
cop
cash
cool
cucumber
cave
cocoa
Cadillac
cow
catcher
corner

D d

dog
dance
dinner
dish
dad
dollars
dime
date
day
dynamite
dud
delicious
dinosaur
diamond
dive

F f

football
feather
finger
fork
food
fat
fish
fudge
family
father
fun
February
fool
fall
fashion

G g

go
guy
girl
gas
gun
gave
gate
gamble
good
gang
gold
game
garden
garage

H h

husband
hurricane
hamburger
hammer
hand
home
hockey
heaven
hell
high
house
hot
hunter
hair

J j

job
junk
Jello
jump
jail
jewelry
jeep
juice
jumbo jet
judge
January
June
July
joker
jam

K k

king
key
kiss
kite
kitchen
kid
kick
kickoff
kangaroo
kitten
ketchup
kidney
kind
keep
kill

L l

lady
lucky
love
line
landlord
little
liquor
lake
log
lunch
ladder
lottery
leg
labor
leaf

M m

mountain
money
man
muscles
machine
mother
movies
music
mud
mustard
McDonald's
microwave
Monday
makeup
magazine

N n

no
nickel
nail
news
Navy
neck
never
nose
net
north
noon
nice
nothing
needle
neighbor

P p

penny
pots
pepper
puppy
paper
paycheck
police
pink
purple
piano
pitcher
pig
pipe
pinball
people

Q q

queen
quarter
quarrel
question
quart
quilt
quit
quiz
quiet
quicksand
quality
quake
quack
queasy
quite

R r

railroad
river
road
rock
radio
rich
red
rat
read
restroom
rainbow
rocket
race
runner
rally

S s

snake
sausage
soap
snowstorm
Sunday
sister
sale
summer
September
skater
south
silver
salt
sixty-six
sun

T t

table
telescope
telephone
toilet
touchdown
tornado
tie
tent
tiptoe
tea
tall
tail
teeth
tunnel
Tuesday

V v

video
valley
valentine
vest
van
vitamin
vet
volcano
vacuum
vanilla
veal
vegetable
vine
vacant
vampire

W w

woman
wet
waves
wash
worm
wine
winter
wire
winner
weekend
work
water
wood
Wednesday
wonderful

Y y

yes
yellow
yesterday
yet
yard
yarn
young
yam
yeast
year
yolk
yogurt
yell
yield
yardstick

Z z

zigzag
zoo
zebra
zero
zeal
zipper
zone
zap
zest
zucchini
zoom
zodiac
zenith
zinc

X x

The words below END with the sound of /x/.

box
tax
ax
six
mix
fox
fix
vex
wax

bl

blood
blind
bluff
blue
bless
blade
blow
blizzard
blossom
blast
blond
blister

cl

clean
cling
clay
clap
close
clothes
closet
clip
climb
clock
clumsy
clue

dw

dwelling
dwindle
dwarf
Dwight
Dwayne

f l

fly
flakes
flee
flame
flag
flap
flat
flow
flu
flare
fling
flavor

br

branch
brain
breath
brook
broad
break
broil
breakfast
broken
bread
bran
brave
braid
bride
bronze
brown

cr

cracker
crumbs
crazy
craft
creative
crayon
crust
creek
creeper
cry
crisis
croak
crucial
crank
crane
crawl

dr

drapes
drive
drove
dream
dress
drag
dryer
dragon
drip dry
drums
drink
draft
drama
dread
drunk
drown

fr

French
fries
freedom
frank
friend
fresh
fried
frozen
frost
freak
from
Friday
frame
Frank
frail
frown

gl

glad
glory
glee
glide
glow
glue
glass
glossy
glance
glamor
glaze
glitter

pl

play
plan
plastic
plywood
plow
plum
please
plate
place
pliers
plane
plague

tw

twin
twelve
twenty
twice
twine
twist
twirl

gr

grapes
greed
gravy
grime
grow
gravity
great
greetings
gripes
groan
group
grease
grateful
gravel
ground
gruel

pr

prince
princess
practice
praise
pretty
preacher
prime
problem
program
profession
promises
pray
private
property
proof
prune

tr

truck
train
trailer
tractor
tree
treat
trip
tribe
trouble
troops
trim
truth
travel
trivia
trick
trespass

sc

scale
scan
scam
scarf
score
scatter
scar
scapegoat
scary

sk

skate
ski
skill
skeleton
sketch
skinny
sky
skirt
skirmish

sl

slip
slide
sleep
sly
slick
sleigh
slime
sling
sleeve

sm

smell
smile
smoke
smart
small
smooch
smuggle
smooth
smash

sn

sneakers
snow
snooze
snake
sneeze
snap
snail
snore
snip

sp

spark
spare
spirit
Spanish
spade
speaker
spit
spider
sponge

squ

square
squeeze
squash
squat
squirrel
squeak
squad
squint
squaw

st

state
sting
steep
stay
stadium
staff
stereo
stain
steam

sw

swing
swim
swear
sweat
swallow
swimmer
swan
sweet
swine
swat

scr

scream
screen
scram
scratch
scramble
scrape
screw
script
scrub

spl

splash
splendid
splinter
splint
split
splurge
splatter
spleen
splice

spr

sprain
spring
spread
sprinkle
spruce
sprocket
sprite
spray
sprout

str

string
street
stripe
strike
straight
strawberry
strap
strategy
strainer

shr

shrink
shrub
shrimp
shrine
shrug
shrill
shred
shrewd

thr

three
thrifty
throw
threw
thread
throne
through
thrill
thrash

ch

children
check
chin
chest
church
cheek
change
cheer

ng

sing
bring
wing
ring
wrong
spring
song
rang

sh

shoe
she
short
shut
shell
ship
shall
shirt
show
shovel
shower
shout
sharp
sheep
shelf
shift
shin
shine
shimmer

th

the
that
this
their
these
them

three
thirty
thing
third
thumb
thunder
thread
thick
thought
thank
Thanksgiving
Thursday

ph

photo
phonics
pharmacy
physician
phrase

wh

white
where
what
when
which
why
wheel
while
whether
whistle

3-D Flashcards

The digraph sounds are sometimes difficult for students to learn, especially ESL students. Using three-dimensional flashcards is a good way to help the student remember the sound. They provide an opportunity to utilize the visual, auditory, and kinesthetic/tactile pathways.

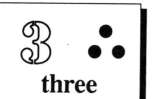

1. Select word to be learned.

2. Print the word on a 5 x 8 flashcard.

3. Glue a physical item to flashcard.

   Student utilizes multisensory approach to learn word.

3-D Flashcards can be easily stored in a regular 5 x 8 card file.

ab

cab	
dab	
gab	
jab	
tab	

ag

bag	rag
gag	sag
hag	tag
lag	wag
nag	

an

ban	pan
can	ran
Dan	tan
fan	van
man	

ack

back	pack
hack	quack
Jack	rack
lack	sack
Mack	tack

all

ball	hall
call	mall
fall	tall
gall	wall

and

band
hand
land
sand

ad

bad	mad
dad	pad
fad	sad
had	
lad	

am

dam	ram
ham	Sam
jam	yam
Pam	

ap

cap	nap
gap	rap
lap	sap
map	tap

ar

bar	jar
car	mar
far	tar

ay

bay	may
day	pay
gay	ray
hay	say
jay	way
lay	

eed

deed	need
feed	reed
heed	seed

ash

bash	lash
cash	mash
dash	rash
gash	sash
hash	

eat

beat	meat
feat	neat
heat	peat
	seat

ell

bell	Nell
cell	sell
dell	tell
fell	well
hell	yell
jell	

at

bat	pat
cat	rat
fat	sat
hat	vat
mat	

ed

bed	red
fed	Ted
led	wed
Ned	

en

Ben	men
den	pen
hen	ten
Ken	yen

end

bend	rend
end	send
fend	tend
lend	vend
mend	

et

bet	net
get	pet
jet	set
let	wet
met	yet

ig

big	jig
dig	pig
fig	rig
gig	wig

ent

bent	rent
cent	sent
dent	tent
gent	vent
Kent	went
lent	

ick

Dick	quick
kick	Rick
lick	sick
Nick	tick
pick	wick

ill

bill	kill
dill	mill
fill	pill
gill	quill
hill	sill
ill	till
Jill	will

est

best	rest
guest	test
jest	vest
lest	west
nest	zest
pest	

id

bid	
did	
hid	
kid	
lid	

im

dim	Tim
him	vim
Kim	
Jim	
rim	

in

bin	pin
din	sin
fin	tin
gin	win
kin	

ob

Bob	lob
cob	mob
fob	rob
gob	sob
job	

og

bog	cog
dog	jog
fog	tog
hog	
log	

ip

dip	rip
hip	sip
lip	tip
nip	zip
quip	

ock

dock	mock
hock	rock
lock	sock

op

bop	sop
cop	top
hop	
mop	
pop	

it

bit	pit
fit	quit
hit	sit
kit	wit
lit	

od

cod	pod
God	rod
mod	sod
nod	

ot

cot	not
got	pot
hot	rot
jot	tot
lot	

ow

bow	row
know	sow
low	tow

uck

buck	puck
duck	suck
luck	tuck
muck	yuck

um

bum	sum
gum	yum
hum	
mum	
rum	

ow

bow	now
cow	sow
how	vow

uff

buff
cuff
muff
puff

ump

bump	lump
dump	pump
hump	rump
jump	sump

ub

bub	pub
cub	rub
dub	sub
hub	tub
nub	

ug

bug	mug
dug	pug
hug	rug
jug	tug
lug	

un

bun	pun
fun	run
gun	sun
nun	

ut

but	jut
cut	nut
gut	rut
hut	Tut

ib

bib
fib
rib
crib

iss

hiss
kiss
miss

y

by
my

ish

dish
fish
wish

ix

fix
mix
six

ee

bee
fee
see
tee
wee

o

go
no
so

ab

crab	scab
drab	slab
grab	stab

ad

Brad
Chad
clad
glad
shad

ail

bail	quail
fail	rail
Gail	sail
hail	tail
jail	wail
mail	frail
nail	snail
pail	trail

ace

face	brace
lace	grace
mace	place
pace	space
race	trace

ade

bade	glade
fade	grade
jade	shade
made	spade
wade	trade
blade	

ain

gain	grain
lain	plain
main	slain
pain	Spain
rain	sprain
vain	stain
brain	strain
chain	train
drain	

ack

black	smack
clack	snack
crack	stack
knack	track
shack	whack

ag

brag	slag
crag	snag
drag	stag
flag	swag
shag	

ake

bake	take
cake	wake
fake	brake
Jake	drake
lake	flake
make	shake
quake	snake
rake	stake
sake	

all

small
squall
stall

amp

camp	clamp
damp	cramp
lamp	gramp
ramp	scamp
tamp	stamp
vamp	tramp
champ	

ane

cane	sane
Jane	vane
lane	wane
mane	crane
pane	plane

am

clam
cram
dram
gram

an

bran	scan
clan	span
flan	than
plan	

ang

bang	sang
fang	tang
gang	clang
hang	slang
pang	sprang
rang	

ame

came	same
dame	tame
fame	blame
game	flame
lame	frame
name	shame

and

bland
brand
gland
grand
stand
strand

ank

bank	clank
dank	crank
hank	drank
lank	flank
rank	Frank
sank	plank
tank	prank
yank	spank
blank	thank

ap

chap	snap
clap	strap
flap	trap
scrap	wrap
slap	

ark

bark	park
dark	Clark
hark	shark
lark	spark
mark	stark

ate

date	rate
fate	crate
gate	grate
hate	plate
Kate	skate
late	state
mate	

ar

char
scar
spar
star

ash

brash	smash
clash	stash
crash	trash
flash	thrash
slash	

ave

cave	wave
Dave	brave
gave	crave
pave	grave
rave	shave
save	slave

are

bare	glare
care	scare
dare	share
fare	snare
mare	spare
rare	square
blare	stare
flare	

at

brat	scat
chat	slat
drat	spat
flat	that

aw

caw	claw
jaw	craw
law	draw
gnaw	flaw
paw	slaw
raw	squaw
saw	straw

ay

bray	pray
clay	slay
cray	spray
fray	stay
gray	stray
play	tray

eam

beam	dream
ream	gleam
seam	scream
team	steam
cream	stream

eet

beet	sheet
feet	sleet
meet	street
fleet	sweet
greet	tweet

eak

beak	creak
leak	sneak
peak	speak
teak	squeak
weak	streak
bleak	

ear

dear	tear
fear	year
gear	clear
hear	shear
near	smear
rear	spear
sear	

ell

dwell	smell
quell	spell
shell	swell

eal

deal	seal
heal	veal
meal	zeal
peal	squeal
real	steal

eep

deep	cheep
jeep	creep
keep	sheep
peep	sleep
seep	steep
weep	sweep

en

wren
then
when

end

blend
spend
trend

ent

scent
spent

est

blest
chest
crest
quest

et

Chet
fret
whet

ew

dew	crew
few	drew
hew	flew
Jew	screw
knew	skew
pew	slew
blew	stew
brew	strew
chew	threw

ice

dice	price
lice	slice
mice	spice
nice	splice
rice	thrice
vice	twice

ick

brick	slick
chick	stick
click	thick
flick	trick

id

quid
rid
grid
skid
slid

ide

bide	chide
hide	glide
ride	pride
side	slide
tide	snide
wide	stride
bride	

ig

brig
sprig
swig
twig

ight

fight	tight
knight	blight
light	bright
might	flight
night	fright
right	plight
sight	slight

ime

dime	clime
lime	crime
mime	grime
time	prime
chime	slime

ine

dine	wine
fine	brine
line	shine
mine	shrine
nine	spine
pine	swine
tine	whine
vine	

ill

chill	spill
drill	still
frill	thrill
grill	trill
skill	twill

in

chin	spin
grin	thin
shin	twin
skin	

ing

bing	cling
ding	fling
king	sling
ping	spring
ring	sting
sing	string
wing	swing
zing	thing
bring	wring

im

brim	swim
grim	trim
prim	whim
slim	

ind

bind	rind
find	wind
hind	blind
kind	grind
mind	

ink

kink	blink
link	brink
mink	chink
pink	drink
rink	shrink
sink	stink
wink	

int

hint	print
lint	splint
mint	sprint
tint	squint
flint	stint
glint	

ive

dive	chive
five	drive
hive	strive
jive	thrive
live	

od

clod
plod
prod
shod
trod

ip

blip	skip
clip	slip
drip	snip
flip	strip
grip	trip
ship	whip

ob

knob
blob
slob
snob

og

clog	grog
flog	slog

it

flit	spit
grit	split
skit	twit
slit	

ock

block	knock
clock	shock
crock	smock
flock	stock
frock	

oke

coke	choke
joke	smoke
poke	spoke
woke	stoke
broke	stroke

old

bold	mold
cold	old
fold	sold
gold	told
hold	scold

op

chop	prop
crop	shop
drop	slop
flop	stop
plop	

orn

born	worn
corn	scorn
horn	shorn
morn	sworn
torn	thorn

one

bone	clone
cone	crone
hone	drone
lone	phone
tone	prone
zone	stone

ope

cope	pope
dope	rope
hope	grope
lope	scope
mope	slope
nope	

ot

blot	shot
clot	slot
knot	spot
plot	trot

ong

bong	tong
dong	prong
gong	strong
long	thong
song	wrong

ore

bore	wore
core	chore
fore	score
gore	shore
more	spore
pore	store
sore	swore
tore	

ow

brow
chow
plow
prow
scow

ow

blow	slow
flow	snow
glow	stow
show	

uff

bluff	snuff
fluff	stuff
gruff	
scuff	

ump

chump	plump
clump	slump
frump	stump
grump	trump

ub

club	shrub
flub	snub
grub	stub
scrub	

ug

chug	slug
drug	smug
plug	snug
shrug	thug

un

shun	
spun	
stun	

uck

Chuck	stuck
cluck	struck
pluck	truck
shuck	

um

chum	scum
drum	slum
glum	strum
plum	swum

ung

hung	slung
lung	sprung
rung	stung
sung	strung
clung	swung
flung	wrung

unk

bunk	flunk
dunk	plunk
funk	shrunk
hunk	skunk
junk	slunk
punk	spunk
sunk	stunk
chunk	trunk
drunk	

ush

gush	brush
hush	crush
lush	flush
mush	plush
rush	slush
blush	thrush

aid

laid
maid
paid
raid
braid

ape

cape   tape
gape   grape
nape   scrape
rape   shape

age

cage   wage
page   stage
rage
sage

air

fair   chair
hair   flair
lair   stair
pair

ard

card   lard
guard   yard
hard

ait

bait
gait
trait

aise

braise
praise
raise

act

fact
pact
tact
tract

alk

balk   chalk
talk   stalk
walk

ant

pant   plant
rant   scant
grant   slant

aft

raft
craft
draft
graft
shaft

ance

dance   glance
lance   prance
chance   stance
France   trance

arm

farm
harm
charm

arn

barn
darn
yarn

arp

carp
harp
tarp
sharp

art

cart	tart
dart	chart
mart	smart
part	start

ase

base
case
vase
chase

ask

ask	task
cask	flask
mask	

ass

bass	brass
lass	class
mass	glass
pass	grass

ast

cast	past
fast	vast
last	blast
mast	

atch

batch	scratch
catch	thatch
hatch	
match	

ax

lax	wax
Max	flax
tax	

aze

daze	blaze
faze	craze
haze	
raze	

ee

knee
flee
glee

ead

dead	dread
head	spread
lead	thread
read	tread
bread	

ean

bean	mean
dean	wean
Jean	clean
lean	glean

eap

heap
leap
reap
cheap

eek

leek	cheek
meek	creek
peek	Greek
seek	sleek
week	

eel

feel	reel
heel	creel
keel	steel
kneel	wheel
peel	

eem

deem
seem
teem

een

queen	screen
seen	sheen
teen	
green	

eer

beer	sneer
deer	steer
jeer	
peer	
queer	

ess

Bess	chess
guess	dress
less	press
mess	stress
bless	

ib

crib

ibe

jibe	tribe
bribe	scribe

ie

die	tie
fie	vie
lie	
pie	

ife

fife
life
wife
knife
strife

iff
cliff
skiff
sniff
stiff

ift
gift	shift
lift	swift
rift	thrift
drift	

ike
bike	Mike
dike	pike
hike	spike
like	strike

ile
bile	tile
mile	vile
Nile	smile
pile	while

ilt
jilt
kilt
quilt
tilt
wilt

ince
mince
since
wince
prince

ipe
pipe	snipe
ripe	stripe
wipe	tripe
gripe	

ire
fire	spire
hire	squire
tire	
wire	

irt
dirt
flirt
shirt
skirt
squirt

ise
rise
wise
guise

ish
swish

isk
disk	frisk
risk	whisk
brisk	

iss
bliss
Swiss

ist	**oach**	**oal**
list	coach	coal
mist	poach	foal
wrist	roach	goal
grist		shoal
twist		

itch	**oad**	**oam**
bitch	load	foam
ditch	road	loam
pitch	toad	roam
witch		
switch		

ite		**oak**	**oan**
bite	site	soak	Joan
kite	white	cloak	loan
mite	write	croak	moan
quite	spite		groan
rite	sprite		

oar

boar
roar
soar

oast

boast
coast
roast
toast

oat

boat   float
coat   throat
goat
moat
bloat

obe

lobe
robe
globe
probe

ode

code
lode
mode
node
rode

ole

dole   pole
hole   role
mole   stole
        whole

oll

poll   scroll
roll   stroll
toll   troll

olt

bolt
colt
jolt
molt
volt

ome

dome
home
Nome
Rome
tome
chrome

ome

come
some

orch

porch
torch
scorch

ork

cork
fork
York
stork

ort

fort   short
Mort   snort
port   sport
sort   tort

ose

hose   chose
nose   close
pose   prose
rose   those

ote

note
quote
rote
vote
wrote

ove

cove
clove
drove
grove

ud

spud
stud
thud

unt

bunt
hunt
punt
runt
blunt
grunt
stunt

ust

bust
dust
just
lust
rust
thrust
trust

aught

caught
taught
naught
fraught

awn

dawn   yawn
fawn   drawn
lawn   prawn
pawn   spawn

eigh

neigh
weigh
sleigh

ief

brief
chief
grief
thief

oil

boil   soil
coil   toil
foil   spoil

oin

coin
join
loin
groin

oo

coo   too
goo   woo
moo   zoo
poo   shoo

ood

good
hood
wood
stood

ood

food
mood
brood

ook

book   took
cook   brook
hook   crook
look   shook

ool

cool   school
fool   spool
pool   stool
drool

oom

boom   bloom
doom   broom
loom   gloom
room   groom

oon

boon	soon
loon	croon
moon	spoon
noon	swoon

oop

hoop	sloop
loop	snoop
droop	swoop
scoop	troop

oot

boot	root
hoot	toot
loot	scoot
moot	shoot

oss

boss	cross
loss	floss
moss	gloss
toss	

ost

cost
lost
frost

ost

host
most
post

otch

botch
notch
blotch
crotch
Scotch

ought

bought	sought
fought	brought
ought	thought

ough

rough
tough
enough

ould

could
would
should

ounce

bounce
pounce
flounce
trounce

ound

bound	pound
found	round
hound	sound
mound	ground

ouse

douse	souse
house	grouse
louse	spouse
mouse	

owl

fowl	growl
howl	prowl
jowl	scowl

ude

dude	crude
nude	prude
rude	

out

bout	spout
pout	sprout
scout	stout
shout	trout

own

down	clown
gown	crown
town	drown
brown	frown

udge

fudge	grudge
judge	sludge
nudge	

outh

mouth	
south	

own

blown	known
flown	own
grown	shown

ue

due	clue
Sue	flue
blue	glue

ove

dove	
love	
glove	
shove	

oy

boy	Roy
coy	soy
joy	toy

ull

dull	lull
gull	mull
hull	

umb

dumb   plumb
numb   thumb
crumb

une

June
tune
prune

urse

curse
nurse
purse

unch

bunch   munch
hunch   punch
lunch   crunch

ur

cur   slur
fur   spur
blur

ute

jute
lute
flute

A
airline
airplane
airport
anthilll
anyone
anyplace
anything
anytime
anywhere
ashtray

B
backbone
backfire
background
backpack
backstage
backwoods
bankbook
baseball
basketball
bathroom
bedroom
bellboy
beside
blackberry
blackbird
blackboard
blackmail
blackout
blacksmith
blacktop
blowout
blueberry
bluebird
bluebonnet
bluecollar
bluefish

blueprint
boardwalk
bridesmaid
buckeye
bucksaw
buckshot
buckskin
bucktooth
bulldog
bulldoze
bullfight
bullfrog

C
candlelight
candlestick
carhop
carload
carport
catbird
catcall
cattail
catwalk
checkbook
checkoff
checkout
checkroom
clubhouse
cowboy
cupcake

D
dogcatcher
dogfight
doghouse
downstairs
downtown
downwind

drugstore
drumbeat
drumsticks

E
earplug
earring
earshot
eyeball
eyedropper
eyelash
eyelid
eyesight

F
farmhand
farmhouse
farmyard
fastback
fingernail
fingerprint
fireball
firebug
firecracker
firefly
fireman
fireplace
fireplug
fireproof
fireside
firetrap
firewood
fireworks
firsthand
flagpole
flagship
flashback
flashlight

flatware
floodgate
floodlight
flowerpots
football
footbridge
foothill
foothold
footlights
footlocker
footloose
footnote
footpad
footpath
footprint
footstep
footstool
footwork
fruitcake
fullback

G

godfather
godmother
gooseberry
grandchild
grandchildren
granddaughter
grandfather
grandmother
grandson
gravestone
graveyard
greenback
greenhouse
Greenland
gunfire
gunman
gunpoint

H

halfback
hallmark
hallway
handbag
handmade
handout
handsaw
handshake
handstand
hangman
hangout
hangover
hardtop
hardware
hardwood
highway
homeroom
homesick
homework
horsepower
hotshot
houseboat
housebroken
houseclean
housecoat
housefly
household
housetop
housewares
housewife
housework
however
humbug
humdrum

I

iceboat
icebox
Iceland
iceman
infield
inside
into

L

ladybird
ladybug
ladyfinger
landlady
landlord
lineup
lipstick
locknut
lockup
longtime
lookout
lowdown
lunchroom

M

madhouse
madman
manhunt
manpower
meatball

N

newsboy
newscast
newsletter
newspaper
newsreel
newsstand
nightclub
nightfall
nightlife
nighttime
nobody
notebook

O

offbeat
offhand
offset
offshore
offside
offspring
outbid
outboard
outcast
outcome
outdated
outdoors
outfield
outfit
outfox
outlaw
outlet
outline
output
outrage
outreach
outside
overcoat
overcome

overdrive
overflow
overhang
overhead
overhear
overlook
overnight
overpass
overpay
oversee
oversleep
overstep
overtake
overthrow
overturn
overview

P

pancake
paperback
pawnshop
paycheck
payday
payoff
payroll
peephole
pickpocket
pickup
pigpen
pigskin
pigsty
pigtail
pillbox
pinstripe
pinup
pinwheel
pinworm
pipeline
placekick
pineapple
pinfeather

pinhole
playback
playbill
playground
playhouse
playmate
playpen
playsuit
plaything
policeman
printout

Q

quarterback
quicksand

R

racehorse
racetrack
raceway
railroad
raincoat
redhead
redwood
restroom
ringleader
ringworm
ripsaw
runway

S

sheepskin
shipmate
shipwreck
shoelace
shoestring

shopkeeper
shoplift
shortcake
shortchange
shortstop
shotgun
showman
sidewalk
silverware
somebody
someone
something
springtime
strawberry
summertime
sunburn
Sunday
sunfish
sunflower
sunlight
sunrise
sunroof
sunset
sweetheart

T

thumbnail
thumbtack
thundershower
thunderstorm
touchdown
turnoff
turnout
turnover
turnpike
turntable

U

undercover
underdog
underdone
underground
underhand
underline
underpass
understand
underwear
upbeat
update
upgrade
uphill
upkeep
uplift
upright
uproot
upset
upstairs
uptight
uptown
upwind

W

wallflower
washbowl
washcloth
watercolor
waterproof
wheelchair
whiplash
windbag
windbreaker
windshield
wintertime
wiretap
wishbone
within
woodchuck
woodland
woodpecker
woodpile
woodshed
woodwork
workbasket
workbench
workbook
workday
workhorse
workout
workroom
workshop
wormhole

Y

yardstick
yearbook
yearlong

Two-Consonant Rule

absent	confine	indent
addict	consent	inject
attic	contest	insect
basket	convict	inside
bedbug	correct	insult
bedpan	costume	into
better	cutback	kitten
bigwig	dentist	ladder
bottom	dirty	lesson
boxcar	discuss	letter
burden	dusty	lumber
butter	elbow	magnet
cactus	fender	manner
campus	filbert	master
carhop	forget	midnight
carpet	forgot	misfit
carsick	fortune	mistake
catfish	funny	Monday
channel	garden	muffin
chimney	garter	mustang
cobweb	goblin	mutter
coffee	gossip	napkin
collide	gunman	number
combat	gunshot	nutmeg
combine	hammer	object
common	happen	order
commute	hiccup	pepper
compact	holly	perfume
compete	hubbub	person
conduct	income	picnic

piston	silly	traffic
plastic	sissy	trespass
pollute	sister	trumpet
popcorn	sixteen	twenty
possum	sudden	under
pretty	suffer	unfit
pretzel	summer	unfold
problem	sunburn	unlock
public	sunlamp	untie
rabbit	sunny	uplift
rescue	sunset	upset
sandal	suppose	velvet
seldom	suspect	window
shabby	target	winter
shotgun	tomcat	witness

Two-Consonants (Advanced)

action	follow	surrender
advertise	forgetful	thunder
afternoon	hamburger	trespassing
buttercup	important	umpire
butterfat	infection	underline
cancel	interfere	unhappy
carpenter	mention	Wisconsin
cartoon	office	yesterday
committee	passenger	
discount	pencil	
entertain	perfect	
establish	princess	
excellent	silverware	
except	success	
fantastic	suddenly	

One-Consonant Rule

baby	human	promote
bacon	humid	recess
bagel	humor	reform
began	item	repeat
bonus	joker	retail
broken	July	retire
china	label	robot
crazy	labor	shady
crisis	lady	shaky
decide	later	shiny
defend	lazy	silent
defrost	local	sober
depart	major	sofa
donate	meter	solo
duty	minor	spider
elect	moment	spoken
equal	motel	student
even	motor	tidy
evil	music	tiger
favor	okay	tiny
female	open	total
fever	over	truly
fiber	paper	tutor
final	photo	vacant
flavor	pilot	zero
focus	polite	
Friday	pony	
gravy	preheat	
holy	preset	
hotel	pretend	

Combination: One/Two-Consonant Rules

agency	November	vacancy
beginning	occupation	volcano
computer	occupy	
conversation	October	
cucumber	paperback	
December	remember	
election	republic	
emergency	romantic	
independent	supervision	
information	tornado	

One-Consonant "OOPS" Rule

cabin	linen	sexy	envelope
camel	magic	shiver	family
chapel	melon	shovel	minister
city	never	solid	president
civic	oven	travel	promise
closet	panic	visit	recognize
cover	polish	wagon	referee
credit	present	beverage	regular
devil	profit	cabinet	salary
driven	river	celery	satellite
ever	robin	closet	satisfaction
exit	second	company	Saturday
habit	secure	discover	several
lemon	seven	eleven	uniform
limit	severe	energy	vanilla

Beginning Sight Word List

a	have	said	was
all	his	some	water
are	is	the	were
as	Mr.	there	what
come	Mrs.	they	who
do	of	this	woman
does	old	to	women
from	on	two	words
give	one	very	work
has	put	want	you

Intermediate Sight Word List

again	could	knew	school
against	country	know	shoe
answer	danger	laugh	should
any	done	learn	somebody
anybody	double	listen	sorry
anywhere	early	live	such
aunt	eight	love	sure
beautiful	enough	many	their
beauty	eyes	most	thought
become	father	mother	through
been	few	move	touch
both	find	Ms.	uncle
build	four	much	view
business	friends	nothing	war
busy	gone	often	watch
buy	great	once	where
Christmas	group	only	which
city	heard	other	whole
color	hour	people	whose
comb	kind	says	world

Advanced Sight Word List

ache	earth	mountain	steak
aisle	error	natural	stomach
although	example	nobody	straight
among	February	ocean	strength
ancient	foreign	orange	sure
angel	front	ought	sword
area	ghost	picture	thorough
avenue	golf	physical	though
bicycle	great	physician	tongue
bouquet	half	piece	tough
break	height	plaid	toward
breakfast	honest	prove	trouble
choir	hymn	rhyme	truth
climb	iron	rhythm	Tuesday
clothes	island	rough	usual
colonel	juice	scene	usually
cough	length	sew	vague
cousin	liquor	soldier	Wednesday
debt	measure	soul	yacht
door	minute	sponge	young

Four of the Hardest Words to Learn by Sight in English.

though

thought

through

thorough

These 100 words (including their variations) make up about 50 percent of all written material in English. The words are ranked in order of frequency of occurrence. The words can be used on flash cards and in sentences to facilitate learning.

1. the	26. or	51. will	76. number
2. of	27. one	52. up	77. no
3. and	28. had	53. other	78. way
4. a	29. by	54. about	79. could
5. to	30. words	55. out	80. people
6. in	31. but	56. many	81. my
7. is	32. not	57. then	82. than
8. you	33. what	58. them	83. first
9. that	34. all	59. these	84. water
10. it	35. were	60. so	85. been
11. he	36. we	61. some	86. called
12. was	37. when	62. her	87. who
13. for	38. your	63. would	88. oil
14. on	39. can	64. make	89. its
15. are	40. said	65. like	90. now
16. as	41. there	66. him	91. find
17. with	42. use	67. into	92. long
18. his	43. an	68. time	93. down
19. they	44. each	69. has	94. day
20. I	45. which	70. look	95. did
21. at	46. she	71. two	96. get
22. be	47. do	72. more	97. come
23. this	48. how	73. write	98. made
24. have	49. their	74. go	99. may
25. from	50. if	75. see	100. part

Contractions are two words combined together with an apostrophe substituting for part of one of the words.

Our spoken language uses shortcuts and simplified forms. Contractions are an example of what happens when we do that. Adult new readers will use contractions as a natural part of their spoken vocabulary and will see them in print.

Contractions are two words combined together with an apostrophe substituting for part of one of the words.

do + not = don't   **we + are = we're**

Common Contractions

Standard Form	Contraction	Usage
am		
I am	I'm	I'm going shopping.
are		
we are	we're	I think we're done.
you are	you're	You're the greatest.
they are	they're	They're in my group.
is		
he is	he's	I know he's working.
she is	she's	She's got blue eyes.
it is	it's	It's not the one I wanted.
what is	what's	What's for lunch?
that is	that's	She knows that's right.
who is	who's	Who's at the door?
there is	there's	I think there's time.
here is	here's	Here's Johnny!
us		
let us	let's	Let's buy apples!

Standard Form	Contraction	Usage
would		
I would	I'd	I'd like a new car.
you would	you'd	I knew you'd be great.
he would	he'd	She wishes he'd leave.
she would	she'd	She'd better not cry.
we would	we'd	We'd like to order pizza.
they would	they'd	I bet they'd know my mom.
have		
I have	I've	I think I've got it!
you have	you've	You've got nice legs.
we have	we've	He said we've got to go.
they have	they've	They've got two children.
not		
can not	can't	I can't find my hat.
do not	don't	Don't go outside.
is not	isn't	It isn't cold today.
will not	won't	They won't like garlic.
should not	shouldn't	You shouldn't bite your nails.
could not	couldn't	Couldn't you find the street?
would not	wouldn't	I wouldn't ride in a plane.
are not	aren't	Aren't you Joan Collins?
does not	doesn't	It doesn't fit anymore.
was not	wasn't	I wasn't at work yesterday.
were not	weren't	Weren't you at the concert?
has not	hasn't	It hasn't rained in days.
must not	mustn't	You mustn't be late.
did not	didn't	She didn't like his attitude.
will		
I will	I'll	I'll see you in the morning.
you will	you'll	I know you'll be fine.
she will	she'll	She'll be home at 5:00.
he will	he'll	You know he'll drive safely.
it will	it'll	It'll be yellow.
we will	we'll	We'll get the right movie.
they will	they'll	She said they'll find it.
that will	that'll	That'll be $10.99.

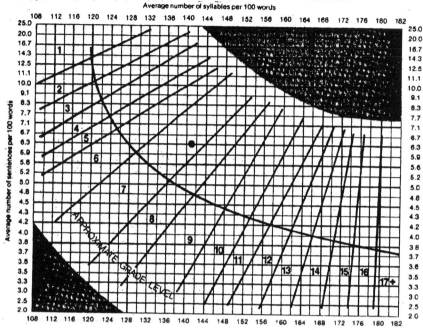

READABILITY 7th Grade (see dot plotted on graph)

Randomly select 3 one-hundred word passages from a book or an article. Plot the average number of syllables and average number of sentences per 100 words on the graph to determine the grade level of the material. Choose more passages per book if great variability is observed and conclude that the book has uneven readibility. Few books will fall in the gray area, but when they do, grade scores are invalid.

Count proper nouns, numerals, and initializations as words. Count a syllable for each symbol. For example, 1943 is 1 word and 4 syllables and ERA is 1 word and 3 syllables.

EXAMPLE:

	SYLLABLES	SENTENCES
1st Hundred Words	124	6.6
2nd Hundred Words	141	5.5
3rd Hundred Words	158	6.8
Average	141	6.3

Directions for Using the Readability Graph

1. Randomly select three samples passages and count out exactly 100 words.

   Begin at the beginning of a sentence.

   Do count proper nouns, initializations, and numerals.

2. Count the number of sentences in the 100 words, estimating the length of the fraction of the last sentence to the nearest tenth.

3. Count the total number of syllables in the 100-word passage. An easy way is simply to put a mark above every syllable over one in each word. When you get to the end of the passage, count the number of marks and add 100.

4. Enter the graph with average sentence length and average number of syllables; plot the dot where the two lines intersect. The area where the dot is placed will give you the approximate grade level.

5. If a great deal of variability is found in the syllable count or sentence count, use more than three samples for your average.

NOTE:

A **word** is defined as a group of symbols with a space on either side. **John, EPA, 1972,** and **&** are each one word.

A **syllable** is defined as a phonetic syllable. Usually, there are as many syllables as vowel sounds. For example, **hopped** is one syllable and **needed** is two syllables.

When counting syllables for numerals and initializations, count one syllable for each symbol. For example, **1917** is four syllables, **RBI** is three syllables.

These examples of manuscript letters are in the traditional format for printing.

Aa Bb Cc Dd
Ee Ff Gg Hh
Ii Jj Kk Ll
Mm Nn Oo
Pp Qq Rr Ss
Tt Uu Vv Ww
Xx Yy Zz

Aa Bb Cc Dd

Ee Ff Gg Hh

Ii Jj Kk Ll

Mm Nn Oo

Pp Qq Rr Ss

Tt Uu Vv Ww

Xx Yy Zz

These examples of manuscript letters are more typical of adult writers.

These examples of cursive letters are more typical of adult writers.

$$Aa \quad Bb \quad Cc \quad Dd$$

$$Ee \quad Ff \quad Gg \quad Hh$$

$$Ii \quad Jj \quad Kk \quad Ll$$

$$Mm \quad Nn \quad Oo$$

$$Pp \quad Qq \quad Rr \quad Ss \quad Tt$$

$$Uu \quad Vv \quad Ww$$

$$Xx \quad Yy \quad Zz$$

ADULTS ONLY
ANTIDOTE

BEWARE
BEWARE OF THE DOG
BUS STATION

CAUTION
CLOSED
COMBUSTIBLE
CONDEMNED
CONTAMINATED

DEEP WATER
DENTIST
DON'T WALK
DO NOT CROSS
DO NOT CROWD
DO NOT INHALE FUMES
DO NOT PUSH
DO NOT REFREEZE
DO NOT SHOVE
DO NOT STAND UP
DO NOT USE NEAR HEAT
DO NOT USE NEAR OPEN
    FLAME
DOCTOR (DR.)
DOWN

DYNAMITE

ELEVATOR
EMERGENCY EXIT
EMPLOYEES ONLY
ENTRANCE
EXIT
EXIT ONLY
EXPLOSIVES
EXTERNAL USE
ONLY

FALLOUT SHELTER
FIRE ESCAPE
FIRE EXTINGUISHER
FIRST AID
FLAMMABLE
FOUND
FRAGILE

GAS
GASOLINE
GATE
GENTLEMEN

HANDLE WITH
CARE
HANDS OFF

HELP	NO FIRES
HIGH VOLTAGE	NO LOITERING
HOSPITAL	NO FISHING
	NO MINORS
IN	NO SMOKING
INFLAMMABLE	NO SPITTING
INFORMATION	NO TOUCHING
INSTRUCTIONS	NO TRESPASSING
	NOT FOR INTERNAL
KEEP AWAY	USE
KEEP OUT	NOXIOUS
KEEP CLOSED AT ALL	NURSE
TIMES	NO SMOKING AREA
KEEP OFF (THE GRASS)	NO STANDING
LADIES	OFFICE
LIVE WIRES	OPEN
LOST	OUT
	OUT OF ORDER
MEN	
	POISON
NEXT (WINDOW) (GATE)	POISONOUS
NO ADMITTANCE	POLICE (STATION)
NO CHECKS CASHED	POST NO BILLS
NO DIVING	POST OFFICE
NO DOGS ALLOWED	POSTED
NO DUMPING	PRIVATE
	PRIVATE PROPERTY

PULL

PUSH

PLAYGROUND

RESTROOMS

RIGHT

SAFETY FIRST

SHALLOW WATER

SHELTER

SMOKING PROHIBITED

STEP DOWN

STEP UP

TERMS CASH

THIN ICE

THIS END UP

THIS SIDE UP

UP

USE BEFORE (DATE)

VIOLATORS WILL BE
PROSCECUTED

WALK

WANTED

WARNING

WATCH YOUR STEP

WET PAINT

WOMEN

ALL CARS (TRUCKS) STOP
ASK ATTENDANT FOR KEY

BEWARE OF CROSS WINDS
BRIDGE OUT
BUS ONLY

CAUTION
CONSTRUCTION ZONE
CURVE

DANGER
DANGEROUS CURVE
DEAD END
DEER (CATTLE) CROSSING
DETOUR
DIM LIGHTS
DIP
DO NOT BLOCK WALK
   (DRIVE)
DO NOT ENTER
DRIFTING SAND (SNOW)
DRIVE SLOW

EMERGENCY VEHICLES
   ONLY
END 45
END CONSTRUCTION
ENTRANCE
EXIT ONLY
EXIT SPEED 30

FALLING ROCKS
FLOODED
FLOODS WHEN RAINING
FOUR WAY STOP
FREEWAY

GARAGE
GATES
GO SLOW

HOSPITAL ZONE

INSPECTION STATION

JUNCTION 101A

KEEP TO LEFT (RIGHT)

LANE ENDS
LAST CHANCE FOR GAS

MERGE
MERGE LEFT (RIGHT)

NO STANDING
NO LEFT TURN
NO PARKING
NO PASSING
NO RIGHT TURN
NO RIGHT TURN ON RED
NO STANDING

NO STOPPING

NO TURNS

NO "U" TURN

NOT A THROUGH STREET

ONE WAY - DO NOT ENTER

ONE WAY STREET

PEDESTRIANS PROHIBITED

PAVEMENT ENDS

PROCEED AT YOUR OWN
   RISK

PRIVATE ROAD

R.R.

RAILROAD CROSSING

RESUME SPEED

RIGHT LANE MUST TURN

ROAD CLOSED

ROAD ENDS

SCHOOL STOP

SCHOOL ZONE

SLIPPERY WHEN WET

SLOW DOWN

SLOWER TRAFFIC KEEP
   RIGHT

SPEED CHECKED BY
   RADAR

STEEP GRADE

STOP

STOP AHEAD

STOP FOR PEDESTRIANS

STOP WHEN OCCUPIED

STOP MOTOR

TAXI STAND

THIS LANE MAY TURN
   RIGHT

THIS LANE ENDS

THIS ROAD PATROLLED
   BY AIRCRAFT

THREE WAY LIGHT

TURN OFF 1/2 MILE

TURN OFF

TRAFFIC CIRCLE

TRUCK ROUTE

WATCH FOR FLAGMAN

WATCH FOR LOW FLYING
   AIRCRAFT

WINDING ROAD

UNLOADING ZONE

USE LOW GEAR

YIELD

YIELD RIGHT OF WAY

Barnell Loft, Ltd.
958 Church Street
Baldwin, New York 11510
(800) 645-6505

Cambridge Book Company
888 Seventh Avenue
New York, New York 10106
(800) 526-0485

Contemporary Books, Inc.
180 North Michigan Ave.
Chicago, Illinois 60601
(312) 782-9181

Fearon Education
David S. Lake Publishers
19 Davis Drive
Belmont, California 94002
(415) 592-7810

Globe Book Company
50 West 23rd. Street
New York, New York 10010
(212) 206-8795

Jamestown Publishers
P.O. Box 9168
Providence, Rhode Island 02940
(800) 872-7323

Janus Book Publishers
2501 Industrial Parkway West
Haywood, California 94545
(800) 227-2375

Literacy Volunteers of America
5795 Widewater Parkway
Widewaters 1 Office Building
Syracuse, New York 13214
(315) 445-8000

Longman Inc.
95 Church Street
White Plains, New York 10601
(914) 993-5000

Michigan Products, Inc.
1200 Keystone Avenue
P.O. Box 24155
Lansing, Michigan 48909-4155
In Michigan (800) 292-1773
Outside Michigan (800) 525-8459

Modern Curriculum Press
13900 Prospect Road
Cleveland, Ohio 44136
(800) 982-8319

New Readers Press
P.O. Box 131
Syracuse, New York 13210
(800) 448-8878

Richards Publishing
P.O. Box 66
Phoenix, New York 13135
(315) 695-7261

Scott Foresman and Company
1900 East Lake Avenue
Glenview, Illinois 60025
(800) 323-5482

Steck-Vaughn Company
P.O. Box 26015
Austin, Texas 78755
(800) 531 5015

Michigan Literacy, Inc.
c/o Library of Michigan
717 W. Allegan P.O. Box 30007
Lansing, MI 48909

Please send _____ copies of **LITSTART**, 2nd Edition Revised, @ $11.95 per book to:

Name _____

Address _____

❑ Please send me a catalog of other Michigan Literacy, Inc. publications and materials.

Make check payable to Michigan Literacy, Inc.
Price subject to change without notice

Michigan Literacy, Inc.
c/o Library of Michigan
717 W. Allegan P.O. Box 30007
Lansing, MI 48909

Please send _____ copies of **LITSTART**, 2nd Edition Revised, @ $11.95 per book to:

Name _____

Address _____

❑ Please send me a catalog of other Michigan Literacy, Inc. publications and materials.

Make check payable to Michigan Literacy, Inc.
Price subject to change without notice

Michigan Literacy, Inc.
c/o Library of Michigan
717 W. Allegan P.O. Box 30007
Lansing, MI 48909

Please send _____ copies of **LITSTART**, 2nd Edition Revised, @ $11.95 per book to:

Name _____

Address _____

❑ Please send me a catalog of other Michigan Literacy, Inc. publications and materials.

Make check payable to Michigan Literacy, Inc.
Price subject to change without notice